TURNING POINT
A COLLECTION
OF SHORT
BIOGRAPHIES

Learning Trends

115 Fifth Avenue New York, NY 10003 (212) 254-2420

TURNING POINT

A COLLECTION OF SHORT BIOGRAPHIES

KENNETH KIESZAK

ABOUT THE AUTHOR

Kenneth Kieszak is Director of the Ethnic Culture Center at John Ericsson Junior High School in Brooklyn, New York. A graduate of Queens College, and an expert teacher of minority problems, Mr. Kieszak has produced material for ethnic studies in all media for use at the Ethnic Culture Center.

staff editor, NANCY CALI
designer, WILLIAM FROST

ISBN: 0-87065-914-6

First revised edition 1975

Copyright © 1973, Learning Trends, a Division of Globe Book Company, Inc.
175 Fifth Avenue, New York, N.Y. 10010

PRINTED IN THE UNITED STATES OF AMERICA   5 6 7 8 9

TABLE OF CONTENTS

GUNTHER GEBEL-WILLIAMS

Sparks came from the wire.
The elephants roared.
The lights went out.
The animals were loose.
What could Gunther do?

the world's greatest act

Waiting for the circus to start The noise and laughter stopped. The sound of crunching (*KRUN-ching*) popcorn was gone. No one moved in his seat.

All was quiet. The lights grew dim. Then a spotlight shone on a man dressed in red. People moved to the edge of their seats. "Ladies and gentlemen! Children of all ages," he said. "You are about to see the best act in the world. In the center ring . . ."

As he spoke, the place lit up with bright colored lights. From far away came the sounds of tigers and horses. The beat of the drum grew louder. Boys and girls jumped to their feet. There were shouts of joy.

In came a long line of giant elephants. The crowd cheered. Riding on the first elephant was a handsome young man. The lights bounced off his gold and green suit. He waved and smiled to the crowd.

The star and his animals arrive

A boy shouted, "There he is! There is the greatest circus star in the world!"

The boy was right. The man on the elephant was the highest-paid star in the Ringling Brothers and Barnum and Bailey Circus. His name was Gunther Gebel-Williams (*GEH-bul — WIL-yumz*).

He led the animals to the center ring. He spoke softly to Nellie, Kongo, and Bengal. Bengal was his 400 pound tiger. Nellie and Kongo were his star elephants.

The crowd waited for the act to begin. Gunther had done this trick many times before. But each time he did it as if it were the first time. Bengal got ready to jump on Nellie's back. Kongo also got ready for Bengal. The tiger was to jump back and forth on their backs. Then came the big finish! It was a pyramid *(PEER-uh-mid).* Gunther

Gunther's famous act

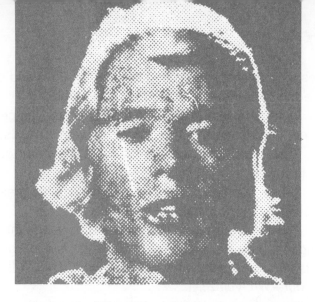

rode on the back of Bengal while the tiger was on Nellie's back. The trio always brought loud appluase (*uh-PLAWZ*).

Gunther was ready. The act was about to start. Nellie moved her giant body around the ring. Bengal got ready to jump.

Trouble in the ring

Then it happened! One of the electrical wires broke. It was touching the metal ring. Nellie's trunk touched the metal. Sparks flew! Nellie jumped back! The 10,000-pound animal was out of control. Nellie charged blindly. She went straight for the door of the cage. There was a loud noise. All at once the lights went out. Kongo and Bengal moved about in the dark. The frightened (*FRY-tend*) animals were loose!

His best act ever

Gunther was alone with the animals. He had no whip or gun. Would he be killed? Would the audience be hurt?

Gunther could hear the animals moving about. Where were they? Was Bengal behind him? Where were Nellie and Kongo?

Every second seemed like an hour. He searched about in the darkness. He called in a soft, calm (*KAHM*) voice.

The star did his job well. His quick, cool thinking saved his life.

The lights came back on. The crowd cheered an act they had not seen. It was his best act ever! The animals were safely back in the cage.

Gunther learned early how to handle problems. *Gunther's*
He had to grow up fast. He was alone at an early age. He *early life*
never knew his parents. When he was young, his mother
left him with a circus.

The Williams' Circus became his new home. The
owners took care of him. Young Gunther Gebel's name was
changed to Gunther Gebel-Williams. The boy liked
circus life. His foster father taught him many tricks.
Gunther liked riding horses the best.

Then, one day, the circus was his. Mr. Williams was *A new circus*
killed in an accident. *owner*

Gunther took over the running of the circus. He
worked hard. Soon, the circus was the best in Germany.

The animal acts of Gebel-Williams became famous.
Many big circuses asked him to come and work for them.
Each time he refused (*ree-FEWZD*).

In 1968, Gunther came to the United States. The *A new country*
Ringling Brothers and Barnum and Bailey Circus got him
to come. They did this by buying the whole Williams'
Circus.

Gunther likes his new country. He lives well. He
likes rock and roll music and expensive *(eks-PEN-siv)*
cars. In his spare time, he plays golf.

Gunther Gebel-Williams is world famous. He has *The future?*
won three circus awards. No other person holds that
honor. Will he win more? Gunther hopes so.

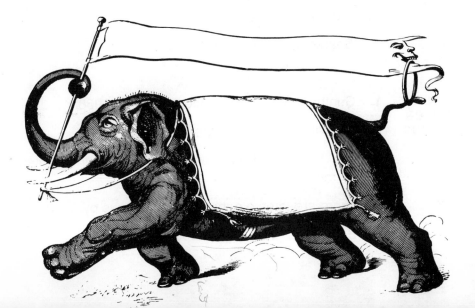

ACTIVITIES

DID YOU GET THE MAIN IDEA?

Gunther proved he was a master showman. He did this by:

    a)   wearing a gold and green costume.

    b)   coming to the United States.

    c)   handling his animals in the dark.

    d)   riding on Bengal.

WHAT IS THE CORRECT ORDER?

1.   The lights go out.

2.   Nellie charges at the cage.

3.   Nellie's trunk hits the wire.

4.   The animals are back in the cage.

5.   The wire breaks.

6.   Sparks fly.

IS IT RIGHT OR WRONG?

1.   Gunther came to the United States in 1968.

2.   Mr. Williams was Gunther's real father.

3.   The Williams' Circus was the best in the United States.

4.   There are three elephants in his famous pyramid act.

5.   Bengal weighed 10,000 pounds.

1. The star elephants were:
   a) Nellie and Bengal.
   b) Gunther and Kongo.
   c) Kongo and Nellie.

2. Bengal was a 400 pound:
   a) elephant.
   b) tiger.
   c) lion.

3. Sparks flew when Nellie touched the wire with her:
   a) foot.
   b) tail.
   c) trunk.

4. Gunther handled the animals with:
   a) a whip.
   b) a gun.
   c) a calm voice.

5. Who left Gunther at the circus?
   a) his mother.
   b) his foster father.
   c) his father.

6. As a young boy, what did Gunther like riding best?

    a) elephants.

    b) horses.

    c) tigers.

7. Gunther was from:

    a) Italy.

    b) the United States.

    c) Germany.

8. When they form a pyramid, Bengal is:

    a) in the middle.

    b) on the top.

    c) on the bottom.

9. The Ringling Brothers and Barnum and Bailey Circus got Gunther to come to the United States by:

    a) asking him.

    b) buying his circus.

    c) giving him cars.

10. Gebel-Williams is the only person to have won:

    a) three circus awards.

    b) two circus awards.

    c) ten circus awards.

DO YOU KNOW THE MEANING?

1. "The lights grew <u>dim</u>." The opposite of dim is:

    a) quiet.

    b) low.

    c) bright.

2. "Then a <u>spotlight</u> shone on a man dressed in red." A spotlight is:

    a) a red light.

    b) a light that shines in a particular place.

    c) an expensive lamp.

3. "It was a <u>pyramid</u>." A pyramid is:

   a) wide at the bottom and narrow at the top.

   b) narrow at the bottom and wide at the top.

   c) wide at the bottom and the top.

4. "The <u>trio</u> always brought loud applause." A trio is made up of:

   a) two things.

   b) three things.

   c) four things.

5. "Nellie charged <u>blindly</u>." Blindly means:

   a) without looking.

   b) with your eyes closed.

   c) feeling your way around.

6. "He had no <u>whip</u> or gun." A whip is:

   a) a pole.

   b) an instrument used to strike animals.

   c) a knife.

7. "He called in a soft, <u>calm</u> voice." A calm voice is:

   a) angry.

   b) peaceful.

   c) loud.

8. "His <u>foster</u> <u>father</u> taught him many tricks." A foster father is a man who:

   a) takes the place of a real father.

   b) is a step father.

   c) adopts a child.

9. "Each time he <u>refused</u>." To refuse means to say:

   a) no.

   b) yes.

   c) maybe.

10. "In his <u>spare</u> time, he plays golf." Spare means:

   a) busy.

   b) extra.

   c) often.

WHAT DO YOU THINK?

1. Why did Gunther speak softly to the animals?

2. Why did Gunther do each trick as if it were the first time?

3. Why did Nellie jump when her trunk touched the metal?

4. Why did Gunther have two last names?

5. Why didn't Gunther carry a gun or a whip?

6. Why did Gunther come to the United States?

HAVE YOU EVER WONDERED?

1. What is life like for a circus star?

2. How many years does a tiger or elephant live?

3. Where do the circus animals stay when they are in the city?

4. Where does the circus go during the winter?

5. What is a *howdah*?

WHAT IS YOUR OPINION?

1. Have you ever seen a circus? Which act did you like best? Why?

2. Have you ever been in a dangerous situation? Tell what happened. Were you cool or were you nervous?

BUFFY SAINTE-MARIE

Producer: This role can make you a star. Do you want the part?
Buffy: I'll take the part if one thing is done.
What did Buffy ask for?

take it or leave it

A call to a television studio

The producer (*pro-DOO-sir*) was in for a surprise. He did not know the young folksinger. Buffy Sainte-Marie (*SAYNT—muh-REE*) was a fighter. She said what she believed. She was proud to be an American-Indian.

Early in 1968, Buffy was called to a television studio (*STEW-dee-oh*). The producer wanted her for his show. The show was called, *The Virginian.* The producer said, "Buffy, we want you in our show. This role can make you a star. Do you want the part?"

Buffy asks for one thing

The young girl stood still. Her long, black hair fell to her shoulders. After a while she spoke. "I'll take the part if one thing is done. I want real actors. The Indians must be real. Do this and I'll be in the show. If you can't, I won't. Take it or leave it!"

The producer thought for a minute. He looked at the girl's dark face. There was no smile. She was not kidding. "All right, Buffy," he said. "You win! We will use real Indians."

The producer answers

Buffy got the part. She also helped write the story.

Buffy brought about a television first. She helped make history. People saw the Indian in his true light.

A television first

This was not her first fight. It would not be her last. It was a small victory. But it was a start. Buffy knew there was more to do.

Buffy wanted to change the image of the Indian. There was a real need for the change. Who was the bad guy? Who was the savage (*SAV-ij*)? Who killed and scalped?

Change the image

For hundreds of years the answer was the same. It was always the Indian.

Buffy had to tell the truth. The lies must stop! The Indian was no savage. He had a proud and rich culture. It was his land that was taken away. His children were killed. He was the one who was forced to leave his home.

The truth

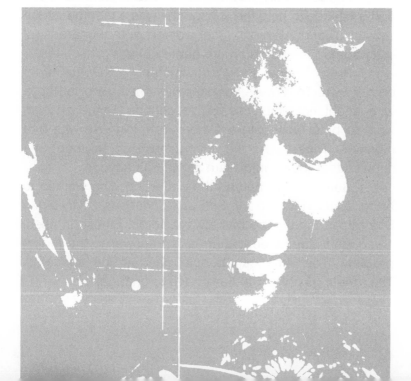

He was made to live on reservations *(rez-ur-VAY-zhunz)*. His life span was twenty years shorter than that of most Americans.

Her problems   Buffy preached this truth. It was not easy. There was so much to do. The lies of the past had to be erased. Movies, television shows, and books had to be changed. But how? How could she change people's thoughts? How could she get people to listen?

Music   The Indian girl tried music. She used her voice and her guitar *(guh-TAR)*. She wrote over two hundred songs. Each told the same story. It was the story of her people. Some songs told of their loss of land. Others spoke of sickness. Many told of the poor schooling. But all told of the suffering of the red man.

Feeling and pain   Buffy sang with feeling and pain. She knew what being poor was. Her early years were spent on a Cree reservation. In her life she has lived on twenty reservations. She knew the real problems of her people.

Other ways she helped   Singing was not the only way she helped. She wrote. Newspapers, books, and magazines told her story. She took many trips. She spoke with many people. At schools and clubs, she told everyone about the Indians.

Buffy works with youngsters   In 1966, Buffy was called to Washington. Here she had a chance to help the young. She was a member of the Upward Bound Project. She worked with hundreds of teen-agers. She helped them get to college.

Her special scholarships   Buffy set up some scholarships *(SKOL-ur-shipz)* on her own. They were very special. They were for those who might not otherwise get to college. Some of them went to bitter youngsters. Others went to those with bad manners. These were the youngsters Buffy helped. She showed that they could learn as well as anyone.

Helping the underdog   Buffy always helped the underdog. She worked to bring equal rights to all. She gave concerts *(KON-sirtz)*. She raised funds. She was always helping those in need.

The future?   Buffy thinks education is the answer to the Indian problem. The American people need to be educated. Their feelings toward Indians have to change.

ACTIVITIES

DID YOU GET THE MAIN IDEA? Buffy helped show the Indian in his true light. She did this by:

    a) joining clubs.

    b) being poor.

    c) living on reservations.

    d) writing a television story.

WHAT IS THE CORRECT ORDER?

1. Buffy is called to Washington.

2. Buffy sees the television producer.

3. Buffy lives on a Cree reservation.

4. Buffy sets up her own scholarships.

5. Buffy gets the part in the television show.

IS IT RIGHT OR WRONG?

1. Buffy was called to do a television show in 1966.

2. Buffy is a Cherokee Indian.

3. The life span of an Indian is twenty years shorter than that of most Americans.

4. Buffy always helped the underdog.

5. Buffy's scholarships were for all high school students.

1. Buffy Sainte-Marie is a:

   a) dancer.

   b) singer.

   c) nurse.

2. Buffy plays the:

   a) guitar.

   b) piano.

   c) drums.

3. As a young girl, Buffy lived:

   a) on a farm.

   b) in a hotel.

   c) on a reservation.

4. Buffy wanted to change the way people felt about:

   a) Negroes.

   b) Indians.

   c) television.

5. The Upward Bound Project helped:

   a) old Indians.

   b) teen-agers.

   c) the producer.

6. One way Buffy got people to listen was by:

   a) giving concerts.

   b) shouting.

   c) living on reservations.

7. The producer wanted Buffy for:

    a) a rodeo.

    b) a television show.

    c) a motion picture.

8. Buffy wanted the producer to use:

    a) real guns.

    b) real animals.

    c) real Indians.

9. Some of Buffy's scholarships went to:

    a) children with bad manners.

    b) blind children.

    c) rich children.

10. A Cree is a:

    a) belief in something.

    b) name of an Indian tribe.

    c) home for Indians.

DO YOU KNOW THE MEANING?

1. "This <u>role</u> can make you a star." A role is:

    a) a plan.

    b) a part in a play.

    c) something round.

2. "She was not <u>kidding</u>." To kid means to:

    a) tell the truth.

    b) act childish.

    c) make jokes.

3. "It was a small <u>victory</u>." The opposite of victory is:

    a) defeat.

    b) win.

    c) success.

4. "Buffy wanted to change the <u>image</u> of the Indian."
Image means:

    a) the way people think about something.

    b) the way something looks.

    c) something make-believe.

5. "Who killed and <u>scalped</u>?" A scalp is:

    a) a sharp knife.

    b) a shrunken head.

    c) the skin on top of a head.

6. "He was made to live on <u>reservations</u>." A reservation
is a place where:

    a) people vacation.

    b) animals live.

    c) Indians live.

7. "His life <u>span</u> was twenty years shorter than that of
most Americans." A span is:

    a) a distance.

    b) a period of time.

    c) the year you are born.

8. "She was a member of the Upward <u>Bound</u> Project."
Bound means:

    a) the direction you are going.

    b) something that is going to happen.

    c) to pull.

9. "Buffy always helped the underdog." An underdog is:

   a) a small puppy.

   b) someone who is not expected to succeed.

   c) someone who is bitter.

WHAT DO YOU THINK?

1. Why did the producer want Buffy to be in his show?

2. Why did Buffy want real Indians in the show?

3. Why was Buffy proud to be an Indian?

4. Why did Buffy live on twenty reservations?

5. Why did Buffy always try to help the underdog?

6. Why were lies told about the Indians?

7. Why did Buffy set up some scholarships?

HAVE YOU EVER WONDERED?

1. How did the first Indians get to North America?

2. What must an Indian boy do to become a brave?

3. How can you tell where an Indian comes from by the way he dresses?

4. Are the Indian nations a part of the United States?

5. How did the Indians get their name?

6. What were scalps used for?

7. What does a producer do?

WHAT IS YOUR OPINION?

1. Many Indians still live in poverty. What can be done to help the Indians?

2. Buffy thinks education is the answer to the Indian problem. Do you think so? Why or why not?

BABE DIDRIKSON ZAHARIAS

Babe did not play well.
She was weak and tired.
She could not go on.
She sat down and cried.
Was Babe's career over?
Had cancer won the battle?

the long road back

The patient is brought back — Four long hours had gone by. Now it was over. The young woman was brought back. She was gently put in bed. The operation was over.

The nurses went to work quickly. The patient (*PAY-shunt*) was given three needles. A tube was placed in her throat. The nurses fixed her pillow.

The doctor wonders — The doctor watched. He looked at the woman in the bed. He wondered. Had he stopped the cancer (*KAN-sir*)? Would she be all right? He looked in the corner of the room. His face grew sad. He shook his head.

The golf clubs — Up against the wall was a set of golf clubs. They belonged to Mildred Didrikson (*DEE-drik-son*) Zaharias. Her friends called her Babe. Babe was a golfer. She was one of the best.

Babe was brave. She made a vow before the operation. "Leave those clubs here," she said. "I'm coming back. I'll be back on the golf course in no time." *Babe's vow*

Would she play again? Few people thought she would. Her operation was very serious. She might never walk again, much less play golf. Her clubs might never be used again. *Her chances*

For five days, Babe lay in bed. She did not move. She was in a deep sleep. Now and then she spoke in her sleep. Sometimes she spoke of golf. Other times her thoughts went back to her childhood. *A deep sleep*

Babe's childhood was full of joy. Her parents had two loves. They loved their children. And they loved America. *Her childhood*

Babe's parents came from Norway. They settled in Port Arthur, Texas. Everything was strange and new to them. They spoke no English. They had few friends. But they loved their new home. *Babe's parents*

The Didriksons showed their feelings quickly. They put up a flagpole. Proudly they raised the flag of their new country. *A new flag*

The family was poor. But the children were happy. They had many things to play with. They had all kinds of sporting goods. Their toys were not store bought. Babe's *Toys from junk*

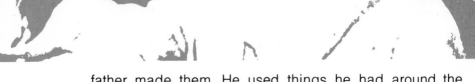

father made them. He used things he had around the house. He turned junk into toys.

The backyard was one large sports arena (*uh-REE-nuh*). There was always something to do. There was a jungle gym. It was made of bars and pipes. There was also a basketball corner. Here, the children played for hours. They shot a ball into a hoop. The hoop was made from a pickle barrel.

Sometimes the boys lifted weights. The weights were also homemade. Two cans of cement were used for ends. The middle was an old broom stick. The younger children swung on a tire. It hung from a tree. One of them sat inside the tire. The other pushed.

The children liked all sports. They played in the winter and the summer. Babe seemed to do well at everything. Football, track, and swimming were some of her favorites. Her baseball hitting earned her a nickname. She was called *Babe* after Babe Ruth!

Golf, however, made her famous. She became the world's best woman golfer. She won the Women's Amateur *(AM-uh-chur)* Golf Championship *(CHAM-pyun-ship)* in 1941. She was the Women's Open Golf Champion in 1948 and 1950.

Now it was 1953. All her struggles *(STRUG-ulz)* in golf seemed small. Now she was fighting cancer. Could she pull through? Could she go back to championship golf? It would be the hardest and longest struggle of her life.

Babe proved she was no quitter. She fought back. Ten days after her operation, she was standing. Everyone was surprised. She was holding her golf clubs again. Five days later she left the hospital.

Many people wrote to her. They sent her thousands of letters. They wished her luck. The letters came from all over the world. Many came from other cancer patients. Her fight became their fight. *Wishes from many*

Babe started her comeback. Many people smiled when they heard. It was one thing to play with friends. It was another to play with professionals (*pro-FESH-un-ulz*). Could she do it? Very few thought she would succeed. *The comeback begins*

It seemed as if the doubters (*DOW-turz*) were right. Babe played in many tournaments (*TOR-nuh-mentz*). She did not do well. She was weak and tired. Once on the golf course she stopped playing. She sat down and cried. It seemed as if nothing would ever go right again. *The doubters*

"Let's call it quits," someone said. "Let's go home and take it easy."

Babe thought for a minute. She knew there were many people counting on her. They wanted her to make a comeback. She knew what she must do. She would not let them down. *Why she went on*

"Let me have the ball," she said. "I'm not giving up!"

Babe went on to win many awards. She won the Women's Open Golf Championship in 1954. She was named "Best Woman Athlete of 1954."

Babe's victory was a victory for all cancer patients. She gave them courage. She brought hope to millions. She helped them on their long road to recovery. *Victory*

ACTIVITIES

DID YOU GET THE MAIN IDEA?

Babe helped many cancer patients. She did this by:

a) giving up golf.

b) having an operation.

c) winning the Open Golf Championship in 1948.

d) giving them courage.

WHAT IS THE CORRECT ORDER?

1. Babe has the operation.

2. The Didriksons put up a flag pole.

3. Babe wins the Women's Amateur Golf Championship.

4. Babe is named "Best Woman Athlete of 1954."

5. The Didrikson's come to the United States.

6. Mildred Didrikson is nicknamed "Babe."

IS IT RIGHT OR WRONG?

1. Babe's parents came from Norway.

2. The Didrikson children had many store-bought toys.

3. Babe went into the hospital in 1954.

4. Her football playing earned her a nickname.

5. Babe was standing five days after her operation.

DO YOU REMEMBER?

1. Babe's operation took:

a) one hour.

b) four hours.

c) ten hours.

2. Babe's married name was:

   a) Zaharias.

   b) Didrikson.

   c) Mildred.

3. What was in the corner of the hospital room?

   a) golf clubs.

   b) a table.

   c) the patient.

4. Outside their house, the Didriksons put up:

   a) a statue.

   b) a flag pole.

   c) a sports arena.

5. Which is not true? The Didrikson children were:

   a) happy.

   b) poor.

   c) sad.

6. The Didrikson children got their toys from:

   a) a store.

   b) a friend.

   c) their father.

7. The younger children played with:

   a) a baseball.

   b) weights.

   c) a tire.

8. Some of Babe's favorite sports were:

    a) baseball and track.

    b) track and soccer.

    c) football and soccer.

9. Babe won the Women's Amateur Golf Championship in:

    a) 1941.

    b) 1948.

    c) 1950.

10. The biggest struggle of Babe's life was:

    a) fighting cancer.

    b) playing golf.

    c) earning her nickname.

DO YOU KNOW THE MEANING?

1. "A tube was placed in her throat." A tube is a:

    a) pipe.

    b) pill.

    c) needle.

2. "Babe was a golfer." A golfer is someone who:

    a) teaches golf.

    b) plays golf.

    c) carries golf clubs.

3. "She made a vow before the operation." A vow is a:

    a) lie.

    b) secret.

    c) promise.

4. "They settled in Port Arthur, Texas." To settle means to:

    a) stay.

    b) leave.

    c) return.

5. "The backyard was one large sports <u>arena</u>." An arena is:

    a) a gymnasium.

    b) an area used for sports or entertainment.

    c) a playground.

6. "They shot a ball into a <u>hoop</u>." The shape of a hoop is:

    a) round.

    b) square.

    c) diamond.

7. "The hoop was made from a pickle <u>barrel</u>." A barrel is:

    a) a large box.

    b) a large container.

    c) a small jar.

8. "She won the Women's <u>Amateur</u> Golf Championship in 1941." The opposite of amateur is:

    a) professional.

    b) best.

    c) beginner.

9. "It seemed as if the <u>doubters</u> were right." To doubt means to be:

   a) sure of.

   b) not sure of.

   c) positive of.

WHAT DO YOU THINK?

1. Why was it hard for the Didriksons when they first came to Texas?

2. Why were the Didkrikson children always happy?

3. Why did Babe have to have the operation?

4. Why did Babe leave her clubs in the hospital room?

5. Why did other cancer patients write her letters?

6. Why did most people think she would never play again?

HAVE YOU EVER WONDERED?

1. Why do people of all ages play golf?

2. What does *par* mean?

3. What is a *birdie?*

4. Why does a golfer yell *fore* to the players in front of him?

5. Why are cancer cells dangerous?

6. Why is it so hard to cure cancer?

WHAT IS YOUR OPINION?

1. Babe's fight against cancer helped other people with the same disease. Do you think that knowing she was helping others made things easier for Babe? Explain your answer.

2. Have you ever helped anyone who has been sick? Who was it? Describe the situation. How did you feel about helping this person?

EDMUND MUSKIE

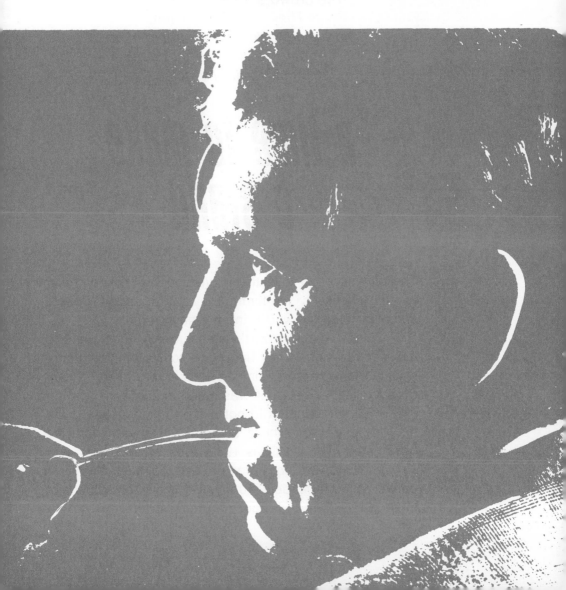

He tried to speak.
The crowd screamed and yelled.
They would not listen.
Edmund Muskie made up his mind!
Today, he would fight back!
What did he do?

a time to make a stand

The crowd
gathers

The crowd began to gather. Some people moved closer to the speaker's platform. They were angry! People shouted, "Stop the war! Bring the boys home!"

The speaker

Many in the crowd were students. They went to the local colleges. They had come to Washington, Pennsylvania for a reason. Edmund Muskie (*MUS-kee*), a candidate for Vice-President, was going to speak.

The angry
students

Some students did not come to listen. They came for another reason. These students were angry with the government. The year was 1968. The war in Vietnam was still on. They were tired of war. They took their anger out on the country's leaders. Today, they would show Senator Muskie what they could do.

The students knew their plan would work. Today would be their day. They would be on television. Newspapers would tell their story. People would find out how they felt.

The student's plan

Signs were made in big letters. Some said, "Stop the war! Get out of Vietnam now!"

One young man laughed. He gave a sign to his girlfriend. "Here," he said. "We'll show this guy. He'll find out what *student power* means. He'll never get a chance to speak."

Student power

The Senator was in his room. From a window, he watched the noisy group below. He listened to the name-calling and the threats *(THRETZ)*.

The senator waits

The name-calling brought back memories. He thought about his childhood. He remembered things he had long since forgotten. He began to daydream.

His childhood

He was back in Rumford, Maine. It was his first day of school. His older sister, Irene, was helping him get

First school day

dressed. His mother was setting the table. His father, Stephen, left his work for a minute. He smiled at his son. This was a big day. The son of a Polish tailor (*TAYL-er*) was going to school.

A father's wish

Mr. Muskie had a secret wish. He hoped his boy would make friends in school. He wanted his son to be accepted (*ak-SEP-tid*).

Not accepted

But Ed had few happy days in school. He was not accepted. The other children called him names. Some of the boys called him names because he was Polish. Others, because he was a Catholic. The name-calling did not stop in class. The boys followed him home. They tried to pick fights with him.

Ed never told his father. He never tried to fight back. Instead, he kept to himself. He played with no one. Edmund Muskie was a boy with no friends.

Never fought back

Suddenly the man was awakened. His daydream ended. There was a knock on the door. "It is time now, Senator," someone said. "The crowd is waiting."

The senator from Maine went to the platform. He stood before the noisy crowd. He tried to speak. The students screamed. He tried again. The same thing happened!

The time is now

Edmund Muskie made up his mind. Today, he would make a stand. He would remain (*ree-MAYN*) silent no longer. He would fight back!

He fights back

The boos and yells stopped. It got quiet. Something Muskie said made the students listen.

The yelling stopped

"Hey, what did he say?" asked one student. "Did I hear right? Did he say he would let one of us speak?"

"Yes, look!" another said. "There goes a student now. He's going on the platform!"

The crowd grew silent. Muskie said, "There is another side to this deed. I will let you speak. You have ten minutes. But you must listen to me for ten minutes. I will hear what you have to say. Then you will hear what I have to say!"

Ten minutes each

The idea worked. Muskie got the young people to listen to him.

History was made in Pennsylvania that day. Young and old listened to each other. Each gave his views.

Young and old together

The speeches ended. Mr. Muskie got the most applause. Those clapping the loudest were the college students. The Polish-American from Maine got his point across.

ACTIVITIES

DID YOU GET THE MAIN IDEA?

Edmund Muskie went to Pennsylvania. He did something different this time. He:

    a)   took a stand.

    b)   gave a speech.

    c)   thought of his childhood.

    d)   received applause.

WHAT IS THE CORRECT ORDER?

1.   Muskie speaks at Washington, Pennsylvania.

2.   Ed spends his first day in school.

3.   Boys pick fights with Ed.

4.   Muskie receives the loudest applause.

5.   The speeches end.

6.   Muskie looks out the window.

IS IT RIGHT OR WRONG?

1.   The war in Vietnam ended in 1968.

2.   Muskie was the senator from Pennsylvania.

3.   Ed had a happy childhood.

4.   Edmund Muskie is a Polish-American.

5.   Edmund Muskie was the Vice-President of the United States.

1. In 1968, Edmund Muskie was running for:

    a) Vice-President.

    b) President.

    c) Senator.

2. The angry students were against:

    a) their teachers.

    b) the Vietnam war.

    c) Polish-Americans.

3. Senator Muskie quieted the students by:

    a) calling in the police.

    b) giving up and walking away.

    c) allowing one of them to speak.

4. Edmund's father was a:

    a) teacher.

    b) senator.

    c) tailor.

5. During his childhood the boys called Edmund names because:

    a) he was Jewish.

    b) he was Irish.

    c) he was Polish.

6. Senator Muskie is from:

    a) New York.

    b) Texas.

    c) Maine.

7. Irene is Edmund's:

    a) older sister.

    b) younger sister.

    c) wife.

8. As a child, Edmund Muskie was:

    a) lonely.

    b) very happy.

    c) well liked.

9. Most of the people who came to hear Muskie speak were:

    a) old.

    b) students.

    c) tailors.

10. When the speeches ended, who got the most applause?

    a) the college student.

    b) the Vice-President.

    c) Senator Muskie.

40

DO YOU KNOW THE MEANING?

1. "Some people moved closer to the speaker's platform." A platform is a:

   a) shoe.

   b) stage.

   c) piece of wood.

2. "They went to the local colleges." Local means:

   a) nearby.

   b) far away.

   c) big.

3. "Edmund Muskie, a candidate for Vice-President, was going to speak." A candidate is someone who:

   a) has won an election.

   b) takes someone else's place.

   c) is running for an office.

4. "He listened to the name-calling and the threats." Threat means to:

   a) hit someone.

   b) say you will do something.

   c) kill someone.

5. "The name-calling brought back memories." A memory is:

   a) something you remember.

   b) something you didn't know.

   c) something funny.

6. "He began to daydream." A daydream is a dream you have:

   a) when you take a nap.

   b) while you sleep.

   c) while you are awake.

7. "The son of a Polish <u>tailor</u> was going to school." A tailor:

   a) makes clothes.

   b) sells material.

   c) cleans clothes.

8. "<u>Suddenly</u> the man was awakened." The opposite of suddenly is:

   a) quickly.

   b) slowly.

   c) quietly.

9. "Each gave his <u>views</u>." Views are:

   a) ideas.

   b) lessons.

   c) speeches.

WHAT DO YOU THINK?

1. Why did the students take their anger out on Muskie?

2. Why did the students think they had power?

3. Why did the students carry signs?

4. Why was Muskie called names when he was a boy

5. Why didn't Ed ever tell his father what happened to him in school?

6. Why did Muskie get the most applause?

HAVE YOU EVER WONDERED?

1. How did the Vietnam war begin?

2. What are some things a candidate has to do?

3. How does a person become a candidate for Vice-President?

4. What are the duties of a Vice-President?

WHAT IS YOUR OPINION?

1. Do you think it is important for government leaders to listen to citizens? Why or why not?

2. Should citizens protest when they disagree with government leaders? Which kind of protest do you think is best? Explain why you think so?

MARIO ANDRETTI

Something was wrong.
The car was out of control!
He tried to turn the wheel.
Nothing happened.
What could Mario do?

a race to death

The race track   There was a smell of gas and burnt rubber. It rose from the sunbaked Phoenix (*FEE-nix*) track. The crowd screamed with delight (*dee-LIYT*). They watched the cars in the distance. The cars seemed to grow larger. They came racing down the track.

The cars get nearer   The cars moved like bolts (*BOWLTZ*) of lightning. They came toward the finish line. They got nearer. The noise of the engines grew louder. They zoomed by. They passed a black and white checkered (*CHEK-urd*) flag. Only one more lap was left. Then the race would be over.

The face of pain   One of the drivers seemed to smile. He was in the lead car.

But it was not a happy smile. It was the face of a man in pain. The heat of the engine went through his gloves and shoes. Giant blisters (*BLIS-terz*) formed on his hands and feet.

The blisters began to break. He held tightly to the steering wheel. He made ready for a sharp turn.

Something was wrong. The car was out of control (*kun-TROWL*)! He tried to turn the wheel. Nothing happened. There was nothing he could do. He was heading straight into a cement wall! *Something was wrong*

Was this to be the end? Would he end up like other drivers? Would he lose a leg or an arm? Was he to end up like his brother? Would his face be smashed up? Would his car catch fire? Would it turn into a flaming coffin (*KOF-in*)? *What would happen?*

The driver seemed to be racing to his death.

The car spun in circles. Driver and car were tossed into the air. There was a loud crashing sound. The car smacked into the wall. The once beautiful piece of machinery was destroyed. It was now a heap of junk. *The crash*

The dust and smoke cleared away. The driver walked away from his car. He acted as if nothing had happened. Mario Andretti did it again. He won his race with death. *The driver comes out*

The Italian-American was not upset. Bruises (*BREW-zes*) and cracked ribs were a part of his life. He returned to the track the next day.

Danger was a part of his life   Danger was part of Mario's life. He came to look for it. "Danger gives life meaning," he said. "There has to be a risk. Every driver must accept it."

His childhood   Mario always liked racing. He grew up with racing in his blood. As a child, he played with toy racing cars. Often his mother found them under his pillow. When he grew older, racing drivers became his heroes. He liked going to the races in Florence, Italy. Racing was his life. He could not keep away from cars and garages.

Secret racing   Mario's father knew the danger in racing. He tried to keep his twins out of the sport. It did not work. Mario and Aldo raced secretly. They entered many junior (*JEWN-yor*) races. Mario was in twenty-five races in one year. He did this when he was thirteen.

A new home   The Andretti family left Italy in 1955. They came to live in the United States.

Something to save for   The boys' interest in racing did not stop. They saved for a car. They worked after school. They worked on Saturdays. Soon, they had enough money. They bought a car. It was old. It did not matter. The boys rebuilt it. They raced their car on the track in Nazareth, Pennsylvania. No one in the family knew. This went on for three years.

Aldo is hurt   Then, in 1959 something happened. Aldo was hurt in a crash. Mr. Andretti was sad and angry. He forbade (*for-BAYD*) the boys to race again.

Mario leaves home   The nineteen year old could not obey. Racing meant too much to him. Mario left home. He did not return until his father let him race.

Mario is accepted   Soon everyone accepted Mario. He became a great racer. If there was a race, he was there. He raced in stock and sports car races. He took part in the Indianapolis Five Hundred and the American and European Grand Prix (*PREE*). He won many of the races. He earned many prizes and titles. Soon he was called "The Fastest Driver in America."

ACTIVITIES

Mario Andretti likes racing. He believes that every driver must accept:

DID YOU GET THE MAIN IDEA?

    a)   crashes.

    b)   cheers from the crowd.

    c)   the risk of danger.

    d)   his car burning up.

WHAT IS THE CORRECT ORDER?

1.   There is a loud, crashing sound.

2.   The driver walks away from the car.

3.   The blisters on his hand begin to break.

4.   The cars pass the checkered flag.

5.   The car goes out of control.

6.   The car spins in circles.

IS IT RIGHT OR WRONG?

1.   Mario was born in the United States.

2.   The cars passed a black and white checkered flag.

3.   Mario only raced in sports car races.

4.   Aldo was hurt in 1955.

5.   As a boy, Mario liked to play with toy trains.

1. The cars passed a black and white checkered flag.
   How many laps were left?

   a) one.

   b) two.

   c) none.

2. The blisters on Mario's hand came from:

   a) the sun.

   b) his gloves.

   c) the heat of the engine.

3. Mario's car went out of control. His car headed
   straight for:

   a) the crowd.

   b) a cement wall.

   c) another car.

4. After the crash his car:

    a) looked the same.

    b) had a few scratches.

    c) was a heap of junk.

5. Mario's mother often found her son's toys under:

    a) his pillow.

    b) his toy chest.

    c) his bed.

6. Mario's heroes were:

    a) movie stars.

    b) baseball players.

    c) racing drivers.

7. Mario's brother Aldo was:

    a) older.

    b) younger.

    c) his twin.

8. When Mario was thirteen he raced in:

    a) 25 races.

    b) 10 races.

    c) no races.

9. The Andretti family came to the United States in:

    a) 1959.

    b) 1955.

    c) 1960.

10. What kind of car did the Andretti brothers buy?

    a) old.

    b) new.

    c) rebuilt.

1. "They <u>zoomed</u> by." To zoom means to pass:

    a) quietly.

    b) quickly.

    c) slowly.

2. "They passed a black and white <u>checkered</u> flag." Checkered means marked with:

    a) squares.

    b) dots.

    c) stripes.

3. "Only one more <u>lap</u> was left." A lap is:

    a) a gallon of gasoline.

    b) a seat in a sports car.

    c) one time around the track.

4. "He was in the <u>lead</u> car." A lead car is:

    a) the car in second place.

    b) the car in front.

    c) the most expensive car.

5. "He held tightly to the <u>steering</u> wheel." To steer means to:

    a) curve.

    b) push.

    c) control.

6. "Would it turn into a <u>flaming</u> coffin?" When something is flaming it is:

    a) fancy.

    b) on fire.

    c) dead.

7. "There has to be a risk." A risk is:

   a) a prize.

   b) a chance.

   c) painful.

8. "They entered many junior races." A junior is some- one who is:

   a) young.

   b) short.

   c) fast.

1. Why couldn't Mario obey his father?

2. Why did Mario like racing?

3. Why did Mario and his brother buy an old car?

4. Why couldn't Mario keep away from cars and garages?

5. Why did the Andretti's come to the United States?

6. Why did Mario's father finally let his son race?

WHAT DO YOU THINK?

1. What happens to a race when a car crashes?

2. How do races help men to design better passenger cars?

3. How is a stock car different from a racing car?

4. How is a racing car built differently from a passenger car?

5. How fast do racing cars travel?

6. When did the first car race take place in the United States?

7. What is the most important car race in the United States today?

HAVE YOU EVER WONDERED?

WHAT IS YOUR OPINION?

1. Would you be willing to accept the dangers of car racing? Do you know of any other sports which involve great risks? Why do you suppose people play in these sports.

2. Do you think Mario was right to race secretly? Would you have done the same thing if your father kept you from doing what you wanted to do? Why or why not?

MARISOL MALARET

The girls waited.
The envelope was opened.
A new Miss Universe was named.
How was a crippled boy the real winner?

the prize money

The contest The Miami Beach crowd stood and cheered. All eyes were on the girl from Brazil. She walked down the brightly lit stage. She was hearing the applause for the last time. Her year was over. On this evening in July her crown would go to someone else. A new beauty would take her place. There would be a new Miss Universe for 1970.

The judges are ready The reporters grew uneasy. The cameramen checked their flashbulbs. Soon they would have their story. The time was near. The judges had just finished. They chose the winner! Soon, a new Miss Universe would be announced (*uh-NOWNSD*).

The waiting The girls on stage waited. They were nervous. The contest was almost over. Only one girl would win. One would get the $10,000 prize money.

The girl from Puerto Rico One of the girls on stage was Marisol Malaret (*MAR-uh-sol MAL-uh-ret*). She came from Puerto Rico.

Marisol was both happy and sad. Talking with the other girls had been fun. She had made new friends. She found out many new things. And she learned about places she never saw. But Marisol was also sad. She missed her aunt and brother. They needed her.

Life had not been easy for Marisol. Her childhood *Marisol's* was not a happy one. There were few happy days. She *childhood* never had a chance to play outdoors. Fun and games were for the other children. Marisol had to stay indoors. The members of her family were sick. She had to take care of them.

There were many things Marisol did not under- *Marisol's* stand. Why didn't she ever go places? Why did her parents *questions* have to stay home? Why was there so little laughter in the house?

Marisol's parents were very sick. They had cancer. *Her parents* When Marisol was nine years old her parents died.

Life was very hard. She had to care for herself *Marisol is* and her brother. His name was Antonio. He was crippled *alone* (*KRIP-uld*).

There was much that had to be done. Who would *Problems* help her? Who would care for her brother? Who would bathe him? Who would carry him out of bed? Who would put him in his wheelchair? These questions were soon answered.

Their aunt came to live with them. She was their *Aunt Esther* mother's sister. Her name was Esther. She was a widow. *arrives* She gave all her love to the children. Aunt Esther became their mother.

Antonio played an important part in their lives. His happiness came first. The two women tried to bring him comfort. After taking care of him, Esther went to work. The money helped. She was able to buy him special medicine. It made life easier for the boy.

Marisol helped at home. She cooked and did the housework. But she always left time for Antonio. She would bring him outside and talk with him. How she wished she could do more! But she could not. There was never enough money. Sometimes they could not even go to church. There was no money for a taxi.

Esther had a dream. It was for Marisol. She prayed her niece *(NEESS)* would finish school. She wanted her life to be different. Maybe she would not grow old so fast. Maybe she would not have to work in a factory.

Marisol did not disappoint her aunt. She worked hard in school. She won a scholarship to the University of Puerto Rico.

For two years Marisol studied. It was not easy. She also worked as a secretary. There was little time for fun. Her hard work paid off. Her aunt's dream came true. She finished with good marks. Marisol was not going to be a factory worker. Better things were in store for her.

Now the past was forgotten. The moment had come. The announcer began to speak. "The new Miss Universe of 1970 is . . ."

Millions waited. They watched their television sets. Soon they saw the beautiful face of the girl from Puerto Rico. Marisol Malaret was the new Miss Universe!

Marisol got a big welcome at home. Some 50,000 persons came to San Juan airport. They came to see the most popular person on the island. They came to cheer Marisol.

Marisol waved to the crowd. "My win," she said "is not just mine. It is yours. My win is a win for Puerto Rico."

Marisol knew there were other winners. They were her aunt and brother.

The prize money would be put to good use.

ACTIVITIES

DID YOU GET THE MAIN IDEA? Marisol Malaret won the Miss Universe Contest of 1970. There were many other winners. All were winners except:

a) Antonio.

b) Aunt Esther.

c) Puerto Rico.

d) Brazil.

WHAT IS THE CORRECT ORDER?

1. Fifty thousand people came to San Juan airport.

2. Aunt Esther came to live with Marisol.

3. Marisol became Miss Universe.

4. The girl from Brazil walked down the stage.

5. Marisol's parents died.

6. Marisol went to the University of Puerto Rico.

IS IT RIGHT OR WRONG?

1. Marisol had a happy childhood.

2. Antonio could take care of himself.

3. Marisol came from Brazil.

4. Marisol won $10,000.

5. Marisol did not work in a factory.

1. The Miss Universe Contest took place in:

   a) Puerto Rico.

   b) Brazil.

   c) Miami Beach.

2. Miss Universe of 1969 was:

   a) Miss Canada.

   b) Miss Brazil.

   c) Miss Puerto Rico.

3. The contest took place in:

   a) July.

   b) January.

   c) September.

4. Marisol's childhood was:

   a) happy.

   b) sad.

   c) fun.

5. When Marisol was nine her:

   a) aunt died.

   b) brother died.

   c) mother and father died.

6. Antonio was Marisol's:

   a) brother.

   b) father.

   c) uncle.

7. Aunt Esther went to work. The money was used to buy special:

   a) food.

   b) medicine.

   c) cars.

8. Aunt Esther did not want Marisol to work in:

   a) an office.

   b) a hotel.

   c) a factory.

9. Marisol went to the University of Puerto Rico for:

   a) four years.

   b) two years.

   c) six years.

10. Some 50,000 people came to cheer Marisol at:

    a) Miami Beach.

    b) San Juan airport.

    c) Brazil airport.

DO YOU KNOW THE MEANING?

1. "A new beauty would take her place." The opposite of beauty is:

   a) pretty.

   b) ugly.

   c) smart.

2. "They were nervous." Nervous means:

   a) uneasy.

   b) calm.

   c) sad.

3. "She was a widow." A widow is:

   a) a woman whose husband has died.

   b) a woman who has never been married.

   c) an aunt.

4. "She walked down the <u>brightly</u> lit stage." The opposite of brightly is:

   a) boldly.

   b) lightly.

   c) dimly.

5. "She prayed her <u>niece</u> would finish school." The opposite of niece is:

   a) daughter.

   b) aunt.

   c) nephew.

6. "Marisol did not <u>disappoint</u> her aunt." To disappoint means to:

   a) make someone unhappy.

   b) pass.

   c) look at.

62

7. "She won a <u>scholarship</u> to the University of Puerto Rico." A scholarship is:

    a) a loan.

    b) an award.

    c) a fee.

WHAT DO YOU THINK?

1. Why was there never enough money in the house?
2. Why did Marisol wish she could do more for Antonio?
3. Why did Esther come to live with them?
4. Why was Marisol happy when she won?
5. Why did Marisol say it was a victory for Puerto Rico?
6. Why did fifty thousand people come to the airport to see her?

HAVE YOU EVER WONDERED?

1. What are some of the things Miss Universe does?
2. How old does a girl have to be to enter the contest?
3. How does a girl get to enter the contest?
4. What are some of the prizes the girls get?
5. Who pays for the gowns and other clothing the girls wear?
6. What happens if the winner gets sick during the year?

WHAT IS YOUR OPINION?

1. Have you ever been in a contest? What kind was it? What was the prize? How did you feel during the contest?
2. If you won $10,000 what would you do with the money?

BOB COUSY

The apartment door opened.
The lights went on.
"Oh no!" the mother cried.
They were everywhere!
What caused the mother to scream?

the new game

The long climb   The family began their climb. They had a long way to go. There were many stairs in their old tenement (*TEN-uh-ment*). The mother stopped. She looked up the winding staircase. She was tired. Her knees hurt from scrubbing (*SKRUB-ing*) the floors that day. She hoped her work would make a difference.

"I hope the spray I bought works," she said.

Mr. Cousy (*KOO-zee*) looked at his wife. He smiled. "We will see, my dear. We will see," he said.

Halfway up the fourth flight she stopped. She rested a minute. "Did I put all the food away?" she wondered. "Yes, I am sure I did," she said to herself.

They reached the fifth floor. They opened the door to their apartment. Young Bob put the lights on.

"Oh, no!" the mother cried. She saw what she hoped she would never see again. They were everywhere. They ran across the table. They moved up the walls. They crawled on the floor. They hid in the cracks and behind the pipes. ROACHES (*ROW-chez*)! There were hundreds of them.

"Oh, it's no use," Mrs. Cousy cried. "We will never be rid of these things. We must get out of here." She held her only son tightly. There were tears in her eyes.

Mrs. Cousy could not get used to New York. Roaches, rats, and bed bugs were now a part of her life. "It was not this way in France," she thought. "Maybe we should have stayed on the farm."

She thought for a minute. She knew she was wrong. "It will soon change," she said. She put her arm around Bob. "Someday son, we will have our own house. There will be trees. There will be grass and clean air."

It took many years for the change to come.

For ten long years the Cousys saved. Mr. Cousy got a job driving a taxi. He worked twelve hours a day. It was hard work. He came home with seventeen dollars each week. The bills were paid first. The money left was put away. Every penny was saved.

Nothing was ever wasted. It seemed as if they had leftovers every night. Bob had to laugh. His mother had a

jar for everything. The leftover coffee was put in a glass jar. The potatoes went in another. Tea bags were dried and saved. They were used over and over. Sometimes the hot water barely turned light orange.

Then the day came. The saving was over. The Cousy family was moving!

They packed what little they had. It was placed into boxes and big paper bags.

Mrs. Cousy wondered. Would her boy miss his old neighborhood? Would he miss the stickball games? Would he miss swimming in the East River? Would he forget the nuns from St. Katherine's?

Bob Cousy looked at the wide open spaces. There were trees, clean streets, and parks. He was happy. He was not sorry they left. He would miss nothing.

Life seemed to start anew. There were many new things to learn. For one, there was a new game. It was called basketball.

Bob liked the game. His large hands seemed made for it. His height (*HIYT*) did not hold him back. His skill came through practice. Soon, he was equal to the tall boys.

Much of his time was spent in the park. He was always at the basketball court (*KORT*). He often had to wait. The bigger boys had to finish their games first. Sometimes he was lucky. The big boys rested. Then he could get in a few minutes of practice.

Bob's friends thought he was a little crazy. Basketball was his whole life. There was no stopping him. Rain or cold made no difference. After a snow, he was on the court. He quickly shoveled (*SHOV-uld*) a path to the basket. The sound of the ball hitting the backboard was heard again. Who was in the park? Everyone knew. It had to be Bob Cousy.

There was no stopping him

Bob's practice paid off. He made the Andrew Jackson High School team. Later, basketball helped get him into college. Bob got a sports scholarship to Holy Cross College.

Practice pays off

Cousy later became a member of the Boston Celtics (*SEL-tiks*). He became known throughout the basketball world. His spirit (*SPEER-it*) and playing made him a star.

The Boston Celtics

He was honored on March 17, 1963. The fans of Boston celebrated "Bob Cousy Day." The star was retiring. He had played for thirteen years. He helped lead his team to five championships in a row.

Bob retires

Bob Cousy made many people in Boston happy. There were many in the sports world who were also happy. They were glad Bob learned to play the new game.

ACTIVITIES

DID YOU GET THE MAIN IDEA? The new game Bob Cousy learned was:

a) stickball.

b) basketball.

c) football.

WHAT IS THE CORRECT ORDER?

1. "Bob Cousy Day" is celebrated.

2. Bob leaves New York City.

3. Bob plays for the Boston Celtics.

4. The Cousys leave France.

5. Bob gets a scholarship to Holy Cross College.

6. Bob learns a new game.

IS IT RIGHT OR WRONG?

1. Bob missed his old neighborhood.

2. The Cousy family took many things to their new house.

3. Bob often had to wait at the basketball court.

4. Bob played for the Celtics for ten years.

5. Bob was very tall.

1. When the Cousys first came to the United States, they lived in a:

    a) tenement.

    b) new house.

    c) farm house.

2. Their apartment was on the:

    a) first floor.

    b) fourth floor.

    c) fifth floor.

3. The Cousys put their lights on. They saw:

    a) roaches.

    b) a robber.

    c) a rat.

4. The Cousys came from:

    a) New York.

    b) France.

    c) Boston.

5. The Cousys bought a house. How many years did they save?

    a) five.

    b) ten.

    c) fifteen.

6. The used tea bags turned the hot water:

    a) brown.

    b) light orange.

    c) green.

7. Bob used to swim in:

   a) the ocean.

   b) the East River.

   c) a pool.

8. Bob used to play basketball in the:

   a) garage.

   b) street.

   c) park.

9. What high school basketball team did Bob make?

   a) Holy Cross.

   b) Saint Katherine.

   c) Andrew Jackson.

10. Bob played for the Boston Celtics for:

   a) thirteen years.

   b) five years.

   c) one year.

DO YOU KNOW THE MEANING?

1. "She looked up the <u>winding</u> staircase." Winding means:

   a) old.

   b) broken.

   c) not straight.

2. "Her knees hurt from <u>scrubbing</u> the floors that day."
Scrub means to:

   a) rub something.

   b) wet something.

   c) dry something.

3. "Halfway up the fourth <u>flight</u> she stopped." A flight
is:

   a) an elevator.

   b) a group of steps.

   c) a hallway.

4. "Nothing was ever <u>wasted</u>." The opposite of wasted
is:

   a) lost.

   b) saved.

   c) thrown away.

5. "Sometimes the hot water <u>barely</u> turned light orange."
Barely means:

   a) naked.

   b) quietly.

   c) just.

6. "His <u>skill</u> came through practice." Skill means:

   a) height.

   b) lessons.

   c) ability.

7. "The sound of the ball hitting the <u>backboard</u> was
heard again." A backboard is:

   a) a fence.

   b) a board behind the basketball hoop.

   c) the floor of a gym.

8. "The star was <u>retiring</u>." To retire means to:

    a) be fired.

    b) quit.

    c) come back.

WHAT DO YOU THINK?

1. Why did Bob's friends think he was a little crazy?

2. Why didn't Bob miss his old neighborhood?

3. Why did Bob practice so much?

4. Why did Mrs. Cousy know she was right in coming to the United States?

5. Why did Bob's large hands help him?

6. Why were many people glad Bob learned to play basketball?

7. Why did it seem like they ate leftovers every night?

HAVE YOU EVER WONDERED?

1. What does *double dribble* mean?

2. What happens when a player travels with the ball?

3. Why is it bad for a player to make more than five fouls?

4. How does a *jump ball* start the game?

5. What is a *foul shot*?

6. How high is the basket?

WHAT IS YOUR OPINION?

1. Has your family ever moved to a new neighborhood? How did you feel when you first moved? What things troubled you? How did you feel after a few weeks?

2. Did you ever save money for something you wanted? What was it? How did you get the money? How did you feel after you bought the thing you wanted?

JIM RYUN

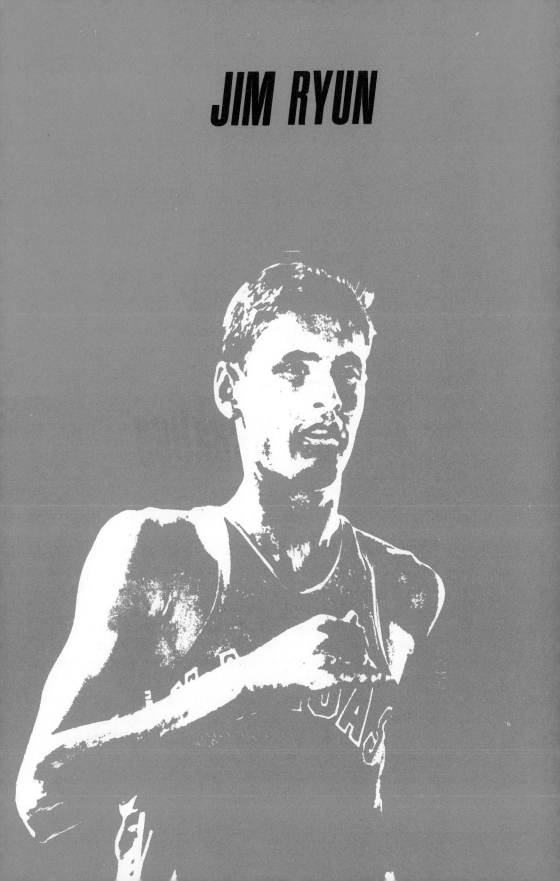

The ball was hit.
It came at him.
Jim picked the ball up.
He threw it with all his might.
What happened to keep Jim off the team?

the weakling

The Little League The boys lined up. Each had his baseball glove ready. Today was a big day in Wichita (*WICH-ih-taw*), Kansas. It was the day for the tryouts. Today a new Little League team would be picked. Eighteen boys would be chosen.

"John Caldwell!" the coach yelled.

The first boy The first boy ran to the field. He waited near third base. He knew he would only be given one chance.

The coach picked up the bat. He hit the ball. John quickly picked it up and threw it.

"All right, John. That was good!" the coach said. "Stand over here."

The coach looked at the list of names. "Jim Ryun!" he yelled. "Jim Ryun, you're next!"

No one answered. No boy went on the field.

The coach yelled again, "Jim Ryun, are you here?"

A young boy was pushed foreward. "That's you silly," another boy said. "Can't you hear? The coach is calling you."

Can't you hear?

Young Jim went on the field. He hoped the coach was not angry. But he did not hear his name. He was slightly deaf.

Jim took his position. He waited. The ball was hit.

Jim waits

Jim picked the ball up and threw it with all his might. But it did not reach first base. In fact, it bounced (*BOWNSD*) three times before it hit the bag.

"Sorry son," the coach said. "Come back next year. Maybe you'll be stronger then."

Maybe next year

Jim put his head down. He walked off the field.

Jim was used to disappointments (*dis-uh-POYNT-mentz*). He did not do well in any sport. He was sick and weak. Most of the time he was in the doctor's office. He had allergies (*AL-ler-geez*). Dust, feathers, and grass made him sneeze.

Allergies

Jim did not give up. He was a fighter. He continued to try out for teams. In junior high school he tried out for the track team. Again, he was disappointed. In high school he tried out again. Once more, he was turned away.

Jim continues to try out

Most boys would have given up. Jim did not. He made up his mind. He would find a way.

Jim's idea
Jim got an idea. He would try out for a team no one else did. He would try out for cross country.

His work really begins
Jim's idea worked. He made the high school cross country team. Now, he had to work extra hard. He had to build his body. This meant practice. Each morning he got up early. Before breakfast he jogged (*JOGD*) for five or six miles. In the afternoon he ran again. He also swam and lifted weights. In the evening he did exercises.

Jim's hard work paid off. He was no longer a weakling. He had turned into a star runner.

A high school runner
Jim became the first high school boy to run a four minute mile. He did this when he was sixteen. When he was seventeen, he broke all records. He ran the mile in 3 minutes and 59 seconds.

Jim had more records to break.

Sportsman of the year
In 1966, Jim was named the greatest sportsman of the year. He deserved (*dee-ZURVD*) it. He broke one United States and two world records. His world records were in the mile and the 1,500 meters. He ran the mile in

3 minutes and 51.3 seconds. He ran the 1,500 meter in 3 minutes and 33.1 seconds. His United States record was in the two-mile run. His time was 8 minutes and 25.2 seconds.

At nineteen, Jim Ryun was world famous (FAY-mus). He was the greatest runner in the history of track.

In 1967, Jim broke his own record. He ran the mile *A new record* in 3 minutes and 51.1 seconds. He was the fastest runner in the world. His fame continued to grow.

Jim's success, however, did not bring him happi- *No happiness* ness. Reporters followed him wherever he went. At home, the telephone rang at all hours. His life was no longer his own. He found himself at the mercy of his fans. They expected (*ex-PEKT-ed*) more and more from him. They came by the thousands to see him. But, they came not to cheer. They came for one reason. It was to see Jim break his record. When he did not, they booed him.

Finally, Jim could take no more. It happened during *Florida* a race in Florida. Halfway through the race, Jim walked off the field. He did not return.

"I want time," Jim said. "I want to live my own life. I need time to rest and relax."

Many called Jim a quitter. Those close to him, *A quitter?* however, knew better. Jim was no quitter. He was a fighter.

Eighteen months went by. Then, in 1971, Jim set *The comeback* foot on a track again. His comeback had begun. By April, *begins* 1972, he had won the Cunningham race. It was for the fifth time. It tied a record. The only person to do so before was Cunningham.

Jim's greatest moment was still to come. It hap- *The Olympics* pened in September of 1972, at the Olympics in Munich, Germany.

When the Olympics began, Jim was there. He was cheered by eighty thousand people. He was one of four runners to bring in the torch.

Jim ran with pride. He held his head high. Across *A proud moment* his chest were the letters U. S. A. It was a proud moment for our country. It was a proud moment for Jim Ryun. The one-time weakling had showed them all.

ACTIVITIES

DID YOU GET THE MAIN IDEA?

Jim overcame being a weakling because:

    a)   he made the cross country team.

    b)   he overcame his allergies.

    c)   he built up his body.

    d)   he took special medicine.

WHAT IS THE CORRECT ORDER?

1.   Jim makes the high school team.

2.   Jim goes to Munich, Germany.

3.   The Cunningham record is tied.

4.   Jim tries out for the Little League.

5.   Jim walks off the track in Florida.

6.   The mile is run in 3 minutes and 51.1 seconds.

IS IT RIGHT OR WRONG?

1.   As a boy, Jim was good in sports.

2.   Jim made the junior high school track team.

3.   Jim jogged before breakfast.

4.   Jim won the Cunningham race four times.

5.   Jim ran for the United States at the Olympics.

DO YOU REMEMBER?

1.   Jim grew up in:

    a)   Florida.

    b)   Kansas.

    c)   Germany.

2. Jim was a sick boy. He had:

    a) cancer.

    b) allergies.

    c) polio.

3. Jim did not make the Little League team because:

    a) he could not hit.

    b) he was late.

    c) he could not throw.

4. Jim made a team when he was in:

    a) elementary school.

    b) junior high school.

    c) high school.

5. Jim ran the four minute mile when he was:

    a) sixteen.

    b) seventeen.

    c) nineteen.

6. To build his body, Jim:

    a) played football.

    b) swam.

    c) played baseball.

7. Jim's running of the mile in 3 minutes and 51.1 seconds was a:

    a) world record.

    b) Olympic record.

    c) United States record.

8. Jim's success made him:

    a) happy.

    b) unhappy.

    c) run faster.

9. Jim returned to the track in:

    a) 1967.

    b) 1971.

    c) 1972.

10. The Olympics of 1972 were held in:

    a) Munich.

    b) Wichita.

    c) Florida.

DO YOU KNOW THE MEANING?

1. "He was slightly deaf." Slight means:

    a) small.

    b) big.

    c) round.

2. "Jim picked up the ball and threw it with all his might." Might means:

    a) practice.

    b) knowledge.

    c) strength.

3. "Dust, feathers, and grass made him sneeze." To sneeze means to let air out:

    a) slowly.

    b) softly.

    c) suddenly.

4. "Before breakfast he jogged for five or six miles." To jog means to:

    a) run very fast.

    b) trot.

    c) walk.

5. "He was no longer a <u>weakling</u>." A weakling is:

   a) strong.

   b) clever.

   c) not strong.

6. "<u>Reporters</u> followed him wherever he went." A reporter works:

   a) at a track.

   b) for a newspaper.

   c) for a store.

7. "Many called Jim a <u>quitter</u>." The opposite of quit is to:

   a) join.

   b) win.

   c) lose.

8. "He was one of the four runners to bring in the <u>torch</u>." A torch is something that:

   a) is lit up.

   b) starts a race.

   c) people stand on.

WHAT DO
YOU THINK?

1. Why were there try-outs for the Little League?

2. Why were the boys only given one chance?

3. Why did Jim spend so much time in the doctor's office?

4. Why wouldn't Jim give up?

5. Why did Jim's idea for getting on the team work?

6. Why did Jim have to work hard to build his body?

7. Why was Jim unhappy with success?

8. Why did people want to see Jim break his record?

9. Why did Jim return to make a comeback?

10. Why did Jim feel proud at the Olympics?

HAVE YOU
EVER
WONDERED?

1. What is a track made of?

2. What kind of shoes does a runner wear?

3. What is the difference between track and field events?

4. How long must a race be to be called cross-country?

5. What are relay races?

6. What is an anchor man?

7. What is the Decathalon?

8. Why do the Olympic games take place every four years?

9. What do the gold, silver, and bronze medals mean?

WHAT IS
YOUR OPINION?

1. Everyone finds some things difficult to do. Describe one thing you had trouble doing? Did you give up?

2. What are your feelings about someone who tries but fails?

JOE NAMATH

He's the best there is!
He's an overpaid flop!
His television shows and movies are great!
He's a terrible actor!
Who is the real Joe Namath?

like him or hate him

The stadium fills   The parking lot was almost full. Still they continued to come. Soon every seat was taken. The stadium (*STAY-dee-um*) was packed. The football game was about to start.

The cheers   The announcer asked for quiet. He called each player by name. Each name brought cheers. One name brought the most cheers. People stood when they heard it. It was the name of a Hungarian-American. He was the star quarterback.

Shouts in the crowd   "He's an overpaid flop," someone yelled. "He's nothing but a cry baby! He should stick to television. At least then you can turn him off!"

"Oh, yeah!" someone answered. "He's the best quarterback in football. He's worth every penny he gets."

A girl in the crowd stood up. She looked at both men. "I don't know much about football," she said. "But this I *do* know. He sure is handsome. Did you see his last movie? . . ."

She did not finish. The players took their positions on the field. The game began.

For the moment the talk was forgotten. But it would start again. This man was interesting. His life was exciting *(ex-SIYT-ing)*. He was Joe Namath.

Joe is known to millions. He is a real superstar. He is known on and off the field. Many know him as a football player. He is the star of the New York Jets. That is not all. He is also in show business. He is often on television shows. He has starred in movies.

The superstar

What makes Joe such a colorful person?

There is a key to Joe's success. It is the way he gets along with people. People either like him or hate him. To many he is a showoff. To his fans he is an idol *(IY-dul)*. "He is today's youth," they say. "He is a man of the changing times."

The key to success

Joe does not care what others think of him. He does what he feels like doing. He says what he thinks. He does not lie. This sometimes causes trouble. "Football is violence *(VIY-uh-lens)*," he once said. "It is not a game. It is people fighting. It is men trying to hurt each other."

He says what he thinks

Joe has been the subject of many stories. His personal life makes good reading. His business dealings are studied. His $10,000 white fur rug has been written about. His scotch drinking is talked about. Even his mustache *(MUS-tash)* has caused concern.

Subject of many stories

Joe's night life　　Joe's night life has caused the most attention. He keeps late hours. He likes night clubs. He is often seen with one or more beautiful girls. "Why aren't you home?" asked a reporter. "Why aren't you resting? There is a big game tomorrow."

Joe was quick to answer. "I'm single and I like girls. I see nothing wrong with that. It doesn't hurt my playing."

$200,000 a year　　Joe makes a lot of money. He makes over $200,000 a year. This has also caused him trouble. Most other players make much less than this. Many players made Joe their target. They were out to get the rich boy.

Joe was always calm. His playing caused many to change their minds. His perfect passes gained him respect. He made many new friends.

No weakling　　The other teams soon learned about Joe. They found he was no weakling. Once he was tackled. His knee was twisted. Joe never said a word. He did not complain (*kum-PLAYN*). The man who hurt Joe was shocked. "This guy can sure take pain," he said. "He must have a body of steel. He acted as if he never felt a thing."

Joe grows up quickly　　Joe learned early not to show pain. He grew up in Beaver Falls, Pennsylvania. There a boy who cried was called a sissy. You had to be rough and tough. You had to be strong. Games were played in junk yards. Gang fights were common.

Joe was the only white boy in the neighborhood. All his friends were black. They all loved sports.

Joe's friends

Being poor did not stop them. They found ways to play. They cleared empty lots. Tin cans and rocks were tossed aside. The cleared fields were used for baseball.

They found a way to play

The boys always kept their gloves and bats handy. Sometimes they had to leave quickly. Quite often a home-run meant a broken factory window. The sound of broken glass meant trouble. The boys ran quickly. They moved in all directions. They knew that the man from the factory moved fast.

The game ends early

The boys also played basketball. They played in the street. A basket was tied to a light pole. Often the game stopped. The boys waited as a car or truck went by. The boys did not mind. When it got dark, they could still play. They used the light from the lamp post.

A night game

The weather did not stop them. They played in rain, heat, and cold. Only the bitter winter stopped them. The game ended when their fingers became numb (*NUM*).

The weather

Joe and his friends stayed together. They went to the same high school. They played on the school basketball team. Again, Joe was the only white boy.

After high school Joe left Pennsylvania. He studied at the University of Alabama. Many of the students called him names. They made fun of him. They did not like Joe's friends.

The University of Alabama

Joe kept his friends. He did not try to change the students' feelings. He knew he could not. "I try to like everyone," he said. "I believe a guy should live the way he wants. If no one is being hurt, I leave them alone. Those guys were brought up differently. I can't tell them what to do. I can't tell them how to live."

Joe's feelings

How do you feel about Joe Namath? Why not read about him. Watch him on television. Then make up your own mind.

How do you feel?

ACTIVITIES

DID YOU GET THE MAIN IDEA?

Joe is a superstar because:

    a) he is a movie star.

    b) he is good in many things.

    c) he is often on television.

    d) he is a great quarterback.

WHAT IS THE CORRECT ORDER?

1. Joe plays on junk heaps.

2. Joe is tackled and his knee is twisted.

3. Joe lives in Beaver Falls, Pennsylvania.

4. Joe gets $200,000 a year.

5. Joe plays on the high school team.

6. Joe goes to the University of Alabama.

IS IT RIGHT OR WRONG?

1. Joe is a Hungarian-American.

2. Joe likes to stay out late.

3. Most football players make about $200,000 a year.

4. Joe was a sissy as a boy.

5. Joe went to the University of Alabama.

1. Someone in the stadium did not like Joe. He said he should stick to:

   a) football.

   b) television.

   c) movies.

2. Joe plays for the:

   a) New York Mets.

   b) New York Jets.

   c) New York Giants.

3. Joe is:

   a) married.

   b) single.

   c) divorced.

4. The key to Joe's success is:

   a) his looks.

   b) his memory.

   c) the way he gets along with people.

5. Joe's white rug cost:

   a) $10,000.

   b) $100,000.

   c) $200,000.

6. Joe said football was:

   a) fun.

   b) violence.

   c) a man's game.

7. All of Joe's childhood friends were:

   a)   black.

   b)   white.

   c)   Chinese.

8. Joe and his friends played basketball in:

   a)   a park.

   b)   the street.

   c)   a gym.

9. Joe went to high school in:

   a)   Pennsylvania.

   b)   New York.

   c)   Alabama.

DO YOU KNOW THE MEANING?

1. "He's an overpaid <u>flop</u>." A flop means something is:

   a)   good.

   b)   bad.

   c)   excellent.

2. "He sure is <u>handsome</u>." The opposite of handsome is:

   a)   ugly.

   b)   good looking.

   c)   beautiful.

3. "What makes Joe such a <u>colorful</u> person?" Colorful means:

   a) alive.

   b) dull.

   c) interesting.

4. "To many he is a <u>showoff</u>." The opposite of a showoff is:

   a) a clown.

   b) a shy person.

   c) a smart person.

5. "Even his <u>mustache</u> has caused concern." A mustache is hair on a man's:

   a) lip.

   b) chin.

   c) cheek.

6. "Many players made Joe their <u>target</u>." A target is something:

   a) left alone.

   b) taken away.

   c) aimed at.

7. "They found he was no <u>weakling</u>." The opposite of weak is:

   a) strong.

   b) tired.

   c) calm.

8. "His knee was <u>twisted</u>." The opposite of twisted is:

   a) crooked.

   b) straight.

   c) broken.

9. "The game ended when their fingers became <u>numb</u>." Numb means:

   a) without feelings.

   b) tired.

   c) wet.

WHAT DO YOU THINK?

1. Why did Joe's name bring the most cheers?

2. Why did the girl talk about Joe's movie career?

3. Why do some people think Joe is a showoff?

4. Why does Joe's private life make interesting reading?

5. Why does Joe get paid so much?

6. Why didn't the other players like Joe?

7. Why did Joe have to be rough as a boy?

8. Why did the students in college feel the way they did?

HAVE YOU EVER WONDERED?

1. Why are some football games not shown on television?

2. How does a player stay in shape?

3. Why do the players wear padding?

4. What is a huddle?

5. What does a quarterback do?

6. How many football players are injured each season?

7. Why do people wear makeup on television?

8. What does video-tape mean?

WHAT IS YOUR OPINION?

1. Do you have a favorite sports person? Who is this person? What do you like about this person?

2. Do you agree with Joe's remark: "I believe a guy should live the way he wants. If no one is being hurt, I leave them alone"? Explain your answer.

THOMAS HOVING

Tom has gone too far this time.
He hit a teacher.
The teacher was knocked out.
We cannot keep him.
You'll have to take him home.
What happened to this trouble maker?

a second home

A long distance call

The telephone rang. The butler answered. "It's for you madam," he said. "It's long distance. It's from New Hampshire (*NEW HAM-shir*). It's someone from Tom's school."

A well-dressed woman got up from a chair. She took the telephone. "Yes, Mrs. Hoving speaking," she said.

Bad news

The man on the other end spoke. "Mrs. Hoving I have some bad news. Your son must go home. He cannot stay here. He is causing trouble. His behavior (*bee-HAYV-yur*) is bad. He must go."

Mrs. Hoving listened quietly. She waited till the principal finished. "What has Tom done?" she asked. "It can't be that bad. Is it?"

Tom went too far this time

The principal spoke. "Yes," he said. "It is very bad. Tom has gone too far this time. He hit a teacher. The teacher was knocked out. We cannot keep him. He is a bad influence (*IN-flew-enss*) for the other boys. You'll have to take him home."

Mrs. Hoving hung up. She looked around the room. *She was alone*
She was alone. She wished there was someone she could
talk to. It was not easy for her. She and her husband were
divorced (*duh-VORSD*). Mr. Hoving left when Tom was
five. Now, Tom was a young man. He was too much for
his mother to handle. He worried her. He was always in
trouble. This was Tom's third school. Now she would
have to find him another. Mrs. Hoving wondered what she
would do.

Young Tom came home. He knew his mother would *Tom came home*
be angry. He tried to talk with her. He tried to explain.
It was no use.

Somehow grownups never understood. "Why was
it?" he thought. "Did they like school when they were
young? Did they ever have fun? What was wrong with
water fights? Why did they get so upset? Didn't they ever
kid around?"

Tom did not like it at home. There was no one to *Bored at home*
play with. He was bored. He got tired of staying indoors.
He hated his apartment. He had to get out!

Tom went to Central Park. It was in the middle of *A second home*
New York City. This was his second home. Here no one

bothered (*BAH-thurd*) him. He could play on the grass. He could run up hills. He could throw rocks into the lake. There were animals to see. There was much to do. Most important, he was free.

At the park, Tom forgot his troubles. Here he was at peace. There were no teachers. There was no homework. There were no tests. Here, Tom was master.

A garden of terror

Twenty years later Tom came back to this park. The park had changed. It was no longer peaceful. It was no longer safe. It had turned into a garden of terror.

Tom was asked to help. He was made the new park commissioner (*kum-MISH-uh-ner*). The Swedish-American was given a big job. He was told to make the park what it used to be.

No easy job

The job would not be easy. When Tom took office, the park was almost empty. It was run down. It was in need of repairs. Mothers kept their children away. They were afraid. Stabbings and beatings were common. Gangs ruled the playgrounds. Dope pushers were everywhere.

Is it too late?

Many thought the park would never be safe. "It is too late," they said. "No one can change this mess. It is impossible."

Tom's answer

Tom did not think so. He had an answer.

The park did not need more fences. Brighter lights were not the solution (*suh-LEW-shun*). People were needed. People would drive away the criminals (*KRIM-in-ulz*). But how could people be brought back into the park?

New ideas

Tom had many ideas. They were new and exciting. They were a mixture of childhood fun and imagination. They were called "Hoving's Happenings."

"Hoving's Happenings"

The "Happenings" soon became the talk of the town. There were Go-Go contests for the young. Fashion shows pleased the women. Children liked the kite-flying contests. The most popular "Happenings" were the concerts. Jazz, rock and roll, and classical music were played.

County living

Tom came up with another good idea. He gave city people a taste of country living. He closed the roads in the park. This was done each Sunday. People could walk through the park. They could ride bicycles. But cars were not allowed. The smell of gasoline and smoke were gone. The air was fresh and clean. The park turned into a large picnic area.

A new job

The commissioner's ideas worked. More than half a million people came back. They rediscovered the park. Crime went down. The park was safe again.

In December, 1966, Tom left his job. He began a new one. He became the director of a big museum (*myoo-ZEE-um*). It was the Metropolitan Museum of Art in New York City.

Tom moved quickly. He opened the museum to all the people. Many old rules were broken. The museum stayed open in the evenings. Tom's personal touch was on everything. His ideas worked. Thousands of visitors came. Once again, the museum was filled with people.

Moving too fast?

Tom's ideas were not always liked. Some thought he was moving too fast. They wanted him to leave things alone. Tom did what he thought was right. He made millions of people happy. He made the museum and the park people's second homes.

ACTIVITIES

DID YOU GET THE MAIN IDEA?
Tom liked Central Park because:
- **a)** of the Go-Go contests.
- **b)** it needed repairs.
- **c)** he felt free there.
- **d)** he was made commissioner.

WHAT IS THE CORRECT ORDER?
1. Tom hits the teacher.
2. The Hovings are divorced.
3. Tom is made director of a museum.
4. Tom is made commissioner of parks.
5. "Hoving's Happenings" are the talk of the town.
6. Mrs. Hoving gets a telephone call from Tom's principal.

IS IT RIGHT OR WRONG?
1. Tom worried his mother.
2. Tom's mother understood him.
3. Tom was a Swedish-American.
4. No one liked the kite-flying contests.
5. Tom became the director of the Museum of Natural History.

1. Tom had to leave his school because:

    a) he failed his tests.

    b) he hit a teacher.

    c) the school closed.

2. Who spoke to the principal first?

    a) the butler.

    b) Mrs. Hoving.

    c) Mr. Hoving.

3. The Hovings were divorced when Tom was:

    a) three.

    b) five.

    c) eight.

4. Tom's second home was:

    a) his apartment.

    b) his school.

    c) Central Park.

5. What did Tom throw into the lake?

    a) rocks.

    b) boats.

    c) paper.

6. The park changed since Tom was a boy. It became:

    a) safer.

    b) less safe.

    c) smaller.

7. Tom's ideas were called:

    a) classical musical.

    b) Go-Go contests.

    c) Hoving's Happenings.

8. Tom closed the park to cars on:

   a) Mondays.

   b) Sundays.

   c) Saturdays.

9. How many people came back to the park?

   a) a million.

   b) half a million.

   c) two million.

10. In December, 1966, Tom left his job. He became:

   a) park commissioner.

   b) director of a museum.

   c) a teacher.

DO YOU KNOW THE MEANING?

1. "The <u>butler</u> answered." A butler is a:

   a) female servant.

   b) male servant.

   c) cook.

2. "He is a bad <u>influence</u> for the other boys." To influence someone means to:

   a) change his ways.

   b) make him disobey.

   c) hurt him.

3. "He was <u>bored</u>." The opposite of bored is:

   a) sleepy.

   b) tired.

   c) excited.

4. "Here no one <u>bothered</u> him." Bother means to:

   a) scold.

   b) play with.

   c) trouble.

5. "Here, Tom was <u>master</u>." A master is someone who:

   a) obeys.

   b) listens.

   c) commands.

6. "It had turned into a garden of <u>terror</u>." Terror means:

   a) fear.

   b) fun.

   c) unhappiness.

7. "He was made the new park <u>commissioner</u>." A commissioner is a person who is:

   a) in charge.

   b) a handy man.

   c) a janitor.

8. "It was in need of <u>repairs</u>." Repair means to:

   a) fix.

   b) buy something new.

   c) paint.

9. "Brighter lights were not the <u>solution</u>." A solution is:

   a) something that is needed.

   b) a problem.

   c) an answer.

WHAT DO YOU THINK?

1. Why did Tom go to school in New Hampshire?

2. Why was Tom a bad influence for the other boys?

3. Why did Mrs. Hoving want someone to talk to?

4. Why didn't grownups understand Tom?

5. Why did the park become his second home?

6. Why did the park change into a garden of terror?

7. Why did Tom's ideas work?

8. Why did crime go down in the park?

9. Why did some people think Tom was moving too fast?

HAVE YOU EVER WONDERED?

1. How do people get a divorce?

2. What causes pollution?

3. How long would it take for the air to become clean again?

4. Are there cars that do not pollute the air?

5. What does the director of a museum do?

6. How big is Central Park?

7. How does the park get the animals for the zoo?

WHAT IS YOUR OPINION?

1. Have you ever been in trouble in school? Describe what happened. What caused the trouble? How did you feel about it? Did you learn anything from it?

2. Describe some of the things you like to do most in parks. What kinds of museums do you like to visit most?

SPYROS SKOURAS

People stopped going.
They stayed home.
The movie houses were empty.
What did Spyros Skouras do?
How did he bring the people back?

the empty seats

Full movie houses

The year was 1945. The movie houses were full. About 90,000,000 people went to the movies each week. The film makers became rich.

Everything changed

For many years the movies did well. Then something happened. People stopped going. They stayed home. The movie houses were empty.

Television

Television had replaced the movies. By 1953, almost everyone had a television set.

The film industry was in trouble. Movie houses began to close. Fewer pictures were made. Many jobs were lost. Film makers and actors were out of work.

The industry fights back

The movie industry fought back. Matinees were shown for children. Stage shows were held on weekends. Theaters gave away dishes and contests became common.

Two new kinds of films were tried. Both brought the screen to life. Special glasses were worn for one. This was 3-D. The other used a special theater. This was Cinerama (*sin-uh-RAM-uh*). *Failure*

The new ideas failed. 3-D films hurt the eyes. Cinerama proved too costly. It seemed as if nothing would work. People still stayed away. The seats remained empty.

Many film makers gave up. They sold their studios. One man, however, did not. He was Spyros Skouras (*SPEE-rus SKOO-ras*). He was the head of 20th Century Fox Studios.

Mr. Skouras was a fighter. He was not one to give up. While others dreamed, he worked. He made his dreams come true. *The fighter*

Spyros's early life was a struggle. His family was poor. Their Greek vineyards (*VIN-yurdz*) produced little. They had barely enough to eat. Yet, they managed. Then, disaster struck! A dam broke near the farm. The water broke loose. It flooded the fields. It left the small farm in ruins. Rocks and sand were all that remained. *Early life*

The boys in the family were sent to work. Money was needed for food. It was needed for another reason. Spyros had five sisters. Each needed a dowry. *Money was needed*

The brothers pitched in. Each did his job. One stayed on the farm. Another went to America. Spyros stayed in Greece. He worked as a printer's apprentice. Later, he worked as an office boy.

His wish   Spyros was unhappy. The work bored him. He wished he was with his brother. "America," he thought, "is for me. There I can be somebody. There I can make my fortune!"

St. Louis   In 1910 Spyros left Greece. The 17-year-old arrived in St. Louis. He joined his brother Charlie. Both worked hard. A 16-hour workday was a part of their lives. They saved all the money they made. In a year they were able to send for their younger brother. Three years later they had saved over $3,000. With that they bought interest in a nickelodeon (*nik-uh-LO-dee-un*). Everything went well. Twelve years later they had an interest in almost every theater in St. Louis.

School   Spyros enjoyed his new country. He was not bored. He could learn new things. Spyros did not just work. He went to school. He took courses in many subjects. He studied for one thing. Someday he would have a career in business.

The Fox Theater   Nothing could stop Spyros. No problem seemed too large to handle. While others gave up, Spyros fought back. The Fox Theater was one example. He bought the bankrupt business. For three years he worked. Soon the business began to improve. Later it was a huge success.

Lucky?   Spyros seemed to do well in everything. Was he lucky? Could he solve every problem? One problem he had to face was television. Could he fight television? Could the movies be brought back to life?

The meeting   Spyros held a meeting. The top film men came. They were all nervous. Spyros looked at the men. He smiled to himself. He knew what they wanted to do. He had seen faces like this before. They all wanted to quit.

The head of the studio stood up. "You may give up if you want," Spyros said. "I will not! I am used to

trouble. Nothing comes easy. We are like men at sea. We are all captains. Our lives are our ships. In a storm we are tested. Many fail. They sink. Those who struggle do not. They come through. Their hard work brings them to port."

Spyros took charge. He worked hard. He knew his job would not be an easy one. "What can I do?" he thought. "How can I compete with television? How can I make the movies better? How can I fill those empty seats?" *No easy job*

Spyros came up with something new. It seemed to make the screen come alive. He called it Cinema-Scope (*SIN-uh-muh-skope*). *Cinemascope*

CinemaScope was different from anything tried before. It was not like a regular movie. A special camera lens was needed. The screen was bigger and curved. The smallest one was 60 feet wide. The sound was stereophonic (*ster-ee-uh-FON-ik*). It came from many speakers. Each was placed in a different part of the theater.

The Robe was the first CinemaScope picture. It opened in 1953. It was spectacular (*spek-TAK-yuh-lur*). The color was vivid. The picture was exciting and beautiful. *The first picture*

Spyros helped other theater owners. He knew they needed money. Their theaters had to be redone. Spyros had his studio give out loans. The credit terms were good. The payments were easy. By 1956 most theaters were equipped for CinemaScope. *Loans*

Spyros's hard work paid off. CinemaScope was a success. Once again the Greek-American had met the challenge. Movies were better than ever. The seats were no longer empty. *No empty seats*

ACTIVITIES

DID YOU
GET THE
MAIN IDEA?
Spyros did well in everything because he:

    a) was lucky.

    b) worked hard.

    c) enjoyed his new country.

    d) was rich.

WHAT IS
THE CORRECT
ORDER?

1. Spyros comes to the United States.

2. Spyros buys interest in a nickelodeon.

3. Spyros works as an office boy.

4. Spyros takes over the Fox Theater.

5. Spyros gets the idea for CinemaScope.

6. The dam breaks on the Skourases' farm.

IS IT
RIGHT OR
WRONG?

1. Spyros had five sisters.

2. Spyros was happy with his work in Greece.

3. Spyros was the first brother to come to America.

4. Spyros settled in Hollywood.

5. The movies did well in 1945.

1. People stopped going to the movie houses because of:

   a) Cinerama.

   b) 3-D.

   c) television.

2. Special glasses were needed for:

   a) 3-D.

   b) CinemaScope.

   c) Cinerama.

3. 3-D failed because it:

   a) hurt the eyes.

   b) was too costly.

   c) used stereophonic sound.

4. Each of Spyros's sisters needed a:

   a) farm.

   b) job.

   c) dowry.

5. How many hours did Spyros usually work a day?

   a) 10.

   b) 12.

   c) 16.

6. Spyros studied to be a:

   a) farmer.

   b) businessman.

   c) film actor.

7. The first CinemaScope picture opened in:

   a) 1953.

   b) 1945.

   c) 1910.

8. *The Robe* was the first movie to use:

   a) Cinerama.

   b) 3-D.

   c) CinemaScope.

9. Spyros helped the theater owners by:

   a) giving them loans.

   b) making new pictures.

   c) buying their movie houses.

DO YOU KNOW THE MEANING?

1. "They sold their studios." A studio is a place where:

   a) movies are made.

   b) movies are shown.

   c) movies are sold.

2. "Spyros's early life was a struggle." To struggle means to:

   a) take it easy.

   b) do your job.

   c) work hard.

3. "It left the small farm in ruins." Something in ruins is:

   a) put together.

   b) destroyed.

   c) almost finished.

4. "Each needed a dowry." A dowry is something brought to a marriage by:

   a) the groom.

   b) the bride.

   c) the guests.

5. "With that they bought <u>interest</u> in a nickelodeon."
To have an interest in something is to:

   a) own all of it.

   b) own some of it.

   c) own none of it.

6. "He was not <u>bored</u>." To be bored is to feel:

   a) no interest.

   b) much interest.

   c) some interest.

7. "They were all <u>nervous</u>." To be nervous is to be:

   a) calm.

   b) scared.

   c) happy.

8. "A special camera <u>lens</u> was needed." A lens is made of:

   a) wood.

   b) glass.

   c) metal.

9. "The color was <u>vivid</u>." Something that is vivid is:

   a) dull.

   b) pretty.

   c) bright.

WHAT DO
YOU THINK?

1. Why was the Skourases' farm left only with rocks and sand?

2. Why did one brother come to America?

3. Why did the sisters need dowries?

4. Why was Spyros bored with his work in Greece?

5. Why did Spyros enjoy America?

6. Why did television keep people at home?

7. Why did many film makers give up?

8. Why didn't Spyros give up on the movies?

9. Why was CinemaScope a success?

HAVE YOU EVER WONDERED?

1. What makes stereophonic sound different?

2. Why is a special theater needed for Cinerama?

3. How do 3-D glasses work?

4. How much film is needed for a one-hour movie?

5. What makes a picture appear on a television screen?

6. What is a television satellite?

WHAT IS YOUR OPINION?

1. Is it easier to do things alone or with others? Is it hard to stand up for something when others do not? Explain your answers.

2. How much time should be spent watching television? Are all shows good to watch?

PATSY T. MINK

The priest raised his arms to pray.
The young girl moved closer to the edge.
The flames grew brighter and higher.
Then, the priest pushed the girl into the crater.
How did Patsy feel about the young girl's death?

two girls from maui

The old man speaks

The old man waited until all eyes were on him. Then he began his story. "Many years ago," he said, "a terrible thing happened. The Great Haleakala (*hal-ee-AK-uh-luh*) volcano (*vol-KAY-noh*) woke up. Something had angered the goddess Pele (*PAY-lay*). She brought sorrow and death to our village."

Pele's anger

"Pele threw up rocks of fire. The sky turned red. It was filled with tongues (*TUNGZ*) of fire. From the bottom of the earth came a burning river. All the beauty you see now was burnt away."

The children were afraid

The children trembled. They moved closer to one another. They were afraid. The old man's story seemed so real. They could almost feel the heat. They could almost see the flames in the volcano.

The sacrifice

The old man continued his story. "The people of Maui (*MAW-ee*) were afraid," he said. "Our priests told us

Pele wanted a sacrifice (*SAK-ruh-fyss*). We threw fruits and animals into the crater (*KRAY-tur*). It did not work. She seemed to get angrier. Our priests told us what we must do."

"The prettiest girl on the island was found. She was dressed in beautiful clothes. Then, she was led to the volcano. The priest raised his arms to pray. The young girl was brought closer to the edge. The flames grew brighter and higher. Then, the priest pushed the girl into the volcano."

The young girl

"Pele was happy. She stopped her fire. The village was saved. Since that day Haleakala has been quiet."

The volcano is quiet

One child was not frightened by this story. In fact, she was angry. "The priests were wrong," she thought. "The girl was killed for no reason. Her life was wasted."

Patsy is angry

Patsy got up. She began to walk back to her village. Then, she stopped. She turned to look at the volcano. "Someday I will help my people," she thought. "But I will not have to die. Alive, I can do more. My life will not be wasted."

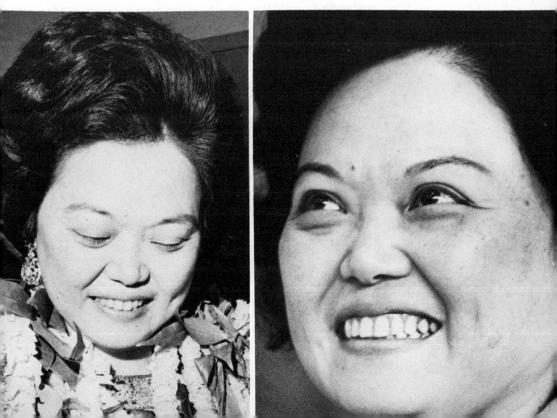

Patsy's island The girl's name was Patsy Takemoto (*TA-kee-moh-toh*). She was born on Maui. She liked living there. It was a beautiful place. The island was alive with color. Beautiful flowers were everywhere. Palm (*PAHM*) trees and waterfalls were always nearby. All around her was a calm, blue-green sea.

Patsy was the daughter of Japanese parents. They had another child named Eugene.

Japanese customs The Takemotos followed many Japanese customs. When they went into a house, they took their shoes off. At mealtime, Patsy's family did not sit in chairs. Instead, they sat on cushions (*KUSH-unz*) and straw mats. They ate simple foods. Their main meal was usually rice and fish. This was eaten with chop sticks. Like most Hawaiians (*huh-WY-anz*), they also ate *poi* (*POY*). This starchy food is eaten with the hands.

The hula Patsy was also proud of being an Hawaiian. As a young girl, she learned to dance the *hula* (*HO-luh*). She was very good at it. Soon, she was the best on the island.

Patsy shared her talent. She taught the other girls in the village. The girls were shown how to move their hips and their hands. She taught them how to move gracefully. Soon, they too were able to dance the hula.

Patsy's childhood Patsy's childhood was a happy one. She found beauty in everything. She loved walking along the sandy beaches. The young girl observed everything. All of nature interested her.

Plants and insects fascinated (*FAS-in-ay-ted*) Patsy. She studied them. Careful records were kept. She

wrote down everything she learned. Her scrapbooks were full of facts. Her room was also full of jars. Each jar was labeled. A different plant or insect was in each jar.

The more she learned, the more she wanted to know. Many questions puzzled her. "How did life begin?" she wondered. "Why are there so many insects? What brings color to flowers? What is the purpose of each living thing?"

Patsy's questions

Pasty continued her studies. In high school, science was her best subject. She learned a lot. Many of her questions were answered. She learned that each thing had a reason for being. One question, however, was still unanswered. "How can I help my people?" she wondered. "I must not waste my life."

Later, Patsy found the answer. She was put on earth to help others. After high school Patsy went to college. She studied to be a doctor. By doing so, she hoped to serve mankind.

Helping others

Patsy changed her mind, however. She studied law instead. "A person in politics," she said, "can do more. He can help many people. He can help to change unjust laws. He can help to make all people equal. The poor and needy can be helped."

Patsy changes her mind

Patsy did not keep her ideas a secret. Before long, her views were known to many. She ran for public office.

The people of Hawaii liked Patsy. In 1958 they elected her to the Hawaiian House of Representatives. In 1962 she became a member of the Hawaiian Senate. In 1964 she went to Washington, D. C. She was elected to the U. S. House of Representatives. Patsy was the first and only Oriental (*or-ee-EN-tul*) woman ever to do so.

Public office

Patsy worked hard. She won the respect of many people. "I bring something different to Congress," she said. "It is my Hawaiian background. I think I can help a great deal. I can help bring an understanding between races."

In Congress

Mrs. Patsy Takemoto Mink helped the people of her islands. She fought for their rights. She won many victories. Her life was not wasted.

The girl from Maui

ACTIVITIES

DID YOU GET THE MAIN IDEA?

Patsy was not like the girl thrown into the volcano because:

a) she was Japanese.

b) her life had not been wasted.

c) she was very beautiful.

d) she danced the hula.

WHAT IS THE CORRECT ORDER?

1. The girl is thrown in the volcano.

2. Patsy is sent to Washington.

3. Haleakala wakes up.

4. Patsy teaches the hula.

5. Patsy goes to college.

6. Patsy becomes a member of the Hawaiian Senate.

IS IT RIGHT OR WRONG?

1. Haleakala was a goddess.

2. Patsy was born on Maui.

3. Patsy had a happy childhood.

4. Patsy's married name is Takemoto.

5. Patsy became a doctor.

DO YOU REMEMBER?

1. The volcano woke up because:

a) Pele was angry.

b) it was hungry.

c) the girl was thrown into it.

2. The volcano was on the island of:

   a) Haleakala.

   b) Pele.

   c) Maui.

3. When the girl was thrown into the volcano:

   a) the sky turned red.

   b) Pele was happy.

   c) rocks of fire came out.

4. When Patsy entered her home, she:

   a) took her shoes off.

   b) put her shoes on.

   c) sat down.

5. Patsy ate *poi* with:

   a) her fingers.

   b) chop sticks.

   c) a fork.

6. Patsy learned to dance the:

   a) waltz.

   b) rumba.

   c) hula.

7. What did Patsy keep in jars?

   a) labels.

   b) insects.

   c) scraps.

8. Patsy believed she was put on earth to:

   a) study nature.

   b) be a doctor.

   c) help others.

9. In high school, Patsy's best subject was:

   a) English.

   b) science.

   c) history.

10. What did Patsy bring to Congress?

    a) a love of nature.

    b) her Hawaiian background.

    c) her scrapbooks.

DO YOU KNOW THE MEANING?

1. "The children <u>trembled</u>." To tremble means to:

   a) shake.

   b) stand still.

   c) jump.

2. "Our priests told us Pele wanted a <u>sacrifice</u>." A sacrifice is something:

   a) offered.

   b) young.

   c) to eat.

3. "Instead they sat on <u>cushions</u> and straw mats." A cushion is like a:

   a) chair.

   b) pillow.

   c) bench.

4. "The young girl <u>observed</u> everything." To observe means to:

   a) look at.

   b) wait on.

   c) enjoy.

5. "Plants and insects <u>fascinated</u> Patsy." The opposite of fascinated is:

   a) interested.

   b) bored.

   c) hate.

6. "He can help to change <u>unjust</u> laws." Something that is unjust is:

   a) strict.

   b) good.

   c) not fair.

1. Why did the old man's story seem so real?

2. Why did the sky turn red?

3. Why did the goddess Pele want a sacrifice?

4. Why did the people listen to the priest?

5. Why is the island of Maui so beautiful?

6. Why did Patsy take her shoes off in her house?

7. Why do some people eat with chop sticks?

8. Why must you be graceful to dance the *hula*?

9. Why did the plants fascinate Patsy?

10. Why was science Patsy's best subject?

11. Why did Patsy change her mind about being a doctor?

WHAT DO YOU THINK?

1. What makes a volcano erupt?

2. What is lava?

3. Why were beautiful children used as sacrifices?

4. Why did many ancient religions use human sacrifices?

5. Why do palm trees grow in Hawaii?

HAVE YOU EVER WONDERED?

6. What do some of the hand movements in the *hula* mean?

7. Why do flowers have different colors?

8. Why are there so few women in Congress?

WHAT IS YOUR OPINION?

1. Many different groups in the United States have special customs. Do you belong to or know about one such group? Can you describe one of their customs?

2. Why is it important for people with different backgrounds to be in politics?

GOLDA MEIR

The horses came rushing down the street.
Chunks of mud flew in the air!
People ran in all directions.
One girl fell. She could not move!
The horses hoofs came crashing down.
What happened to the little girl?

never again

A happy sound

A happy sound filled the muddy street of Pinsk, Russia. People smiled when they heard it. It made them happy. It made them forget their troubles.

Everyone liked to watch the little children play. They always seemed happy. They did not know of trouble. Their laughter seemed to hide the dirt. Disease (*duh-ZEES*) and suffering were not their worries.

The Cossacks

Suddenly someone shouted, "Children! Get out of the street. Quick! Run! Hide! The Cossacks are coming!"

Killers

The Cossacks were feared by Jews. These horsemen were cruel *(KREW-el)!* They were killers! No Jew was safe as they rode through the streets. To be found on the street meant trouble. Jews were beaten. They were whipped and stabbed.

People ran about. They looked for a place to hide. They went inside their homes. Doors were locked. Windows were bolted.

One girl fell

The noisy street grew quiet. The crowds were gone. Some children were still in the street. They rushed to run away. One girl fell. She could not get up. She lay in the mud.

The horses

The little girl prayed. She hoped she would not be killed. The sound of the hoofs grew louder. The horses came rushing down the muddy street.

Chunks of mud flew in the air. The horses were above her. Their hoofs of death crashed to the ground. She screamed! It was no use. No one could hear.

The horses jumped. Their riders stopped. The Cossacks played a game. They moved around the girl's head. Each one tried to come closest. They laughed as they played. The sound was deafening (*DEF-ning*). It was a mixture of screams and laughter.

The game

The girl kept her eyes closed. She was afraid. She did not move or look up. Then suddenly it was quiet. The Cossacks were gone.

They were gone

The girl got up slowly. She looked around. Her prayers had been answered. She was not hurt this time.

The pretty six year old stood up. She could not move. Her eyes stayed on the road. She watched the Cossacks ride farther and farther away. Tears rolled down her cheeks. "This must never happen again," she thought. "No one should ever put his face in the mud."

The girl walked home. Two words kept coming from her lips. She said them over and over. "Never again! Never again!"

Never again

The girl had a dream. Someday it would come true. She would help build a new country. It would be a country where Jewish children would be free. She wanted a place where they could live without fear. The country was Israel. The girl was Golda Meir (*GOL-da my-EAR*).

A dream

Golda did not stay in Russia. She left when she was eight years old. She came to live in the United States.

The United States

Golda's father had come before her. For three years he worked. He saved all he could. Then he sent for his family. His wife and three daughters crossed the ocean. They arrived in New York.

The family was poor. They lived in a one-room apartment. It was in Milwaukee (*mil-WAW-kee*). Later they rented a store. It had two rooms in the back.

Everyone worked hard. Parents and children helped out. The father worked as a carpenter (*KAR-pen-tor*). The mother cared for the small grocery store. The children worked after school. They worked in factories and department stores.

Everyone worked

They did not make much money. They had just enough to pay the rent and buy a little food.

Although poor, two things made them happy. Here, they were no longer afraid. They did not have to fear the police. They did not need to lock their windows and doors. There were no Cossacks. Most important, they could worship as they pleased. No one stopped them. They could practice their religion in peace.

Golda wanted an education (ed-ju-KAY-shun). Her parents, however, were against it. They did not think it was important.

Many times Golda was late for school. It was not her fault. Her mother would not let her go. She was made to work in the store. Golda tried to talk with her mother. She told her she would get into trouble. Her mother did not care. "Education is for boys," she said. "A girl should stay home. She should worry about getting married."

Golda's lateness did not stop her. She graduated (GRAD-you-ay-ted) at the top of her class. She wanted to become a teacher. Once again, her parents tried to stop her. They were afraid she would never get married. She was told no! She could not become a teacher.

Golda found a way to go to school. In the day she worked in a department store. In the evening she taught English to immigrants (IM-uh-grentz). She saved her money. Once she had enough, she left home. She lived with her married sister in Denver.

Here she made new friends. They interested her. They spoke of making a home for the Jews.

Golda saw her chance. Their dream was her dream. Working together they could make it come true.

Golda left the United States. She had lived there for fifteen years. She went to Palestine. Here she worked. She helped build a new country.

Golda's dream came true. It was not just her dream. It was the dream of millions of Jews. On May 15, 1948 they had a home. It was a Jewish country. A new flag was raised. It was blue and white. The Star of David was on it. It flew over Israel.

ACTIVITIES

Golda Meir wanted to build a country where:

DID YOU
GET THE
MAIN IDEA?

- **a)** Jews would be free.
- **b)** there were no Cossacks.
- **c)** children could play.
- **d)** education was free.

WHAT IS
THE CORRECT
ORDER?

1. Israel became a state.
2. Golda left the United States.
3. Golda left Russia.
4. Golda fell in the street.
5. Golda went to Denver.
6. Golda graduated from school in Milwaukee.

IS IT
RIGHT OR
WRONG?

1. Golda's father was a carpenter.
2. Golda was late for school many times.
3. The Cossacks were friendly to everyone.
4. Golda wanted to be a doctor.
5. Golda was born on May 15, 1948.

DO YOU
REMEMBER?

1. The streets in Pinsk, Russia were made of:
    - **a)** dirt.
    - **b)** cement.
    - **c)** tar.

2. The Cossacks were:
    - **a)** Jews.
    - **b)** horsemen.
    - **c)** children.

3. Golda's dream was to:
   a) get married.

   b) leave Russia.

   c) make a new country.

4. Golda left Russia when she was:
   a) six.

   b) eight.

   c) three.

5. Golda's father came to the United States:
   a) three years before Golda.

   b) three years after Golda.

   c) with the family.

6. Golda's family rented a store in:
   a) Palestine.

   b) Milwaukee.

   c) Pinsk.

7. Golda wanted to become a:
   a) teacher.

   b) Cossack.

   c) Jew.

8. Golda taught English to:
   a) immigrants.

   b) children.

   c) Cossacks.

9. Golda lived in the United States for:
   a) five years.

   b) ten years.

   c) fifteen years.

10. The flag of Israel is:
    a) red, white, and blue.

    b) blue and white.

    c) gold.

1. "Windows were <u>bolted</u>." A bolted window is one that is:

    a) open.

    b) locked.

    c) broken.

2. "The sound of the <u>hoofs</u> grew louder." Hoofs are horses':

    a) feet.

    b) eyes.

    c) teeth.

3. "The sound was <u>deafening</u>." A deafening sound is a sound that is:

    a) very loud.

    b) very soft.

    c) not heard.

4. "Her father worked as a <u>carpenter</u>." A carpenter is a person who works with:

    a) metal.

    b) wood.

    c) plastic.

5. "They worked in <u>factories</u> and department stores." A factory is a place where things are:

    a) made.

    b) sold.

    c) taken.

6. "It was not her <u>fault</u>." A fault is a:

    a) problem.

    b) mistake.

    c) worry.

7. "In the evening she taught English to <u>immigrants</u>."
   An immigrant is a person who:

   a) leaves the country of his birth.

   b) comes to America.

   c) visits another country.

WHAT DO YOU THINK?

1. Why didn't the children know of trouble?

2. Why did people like to watch the children play?

3. Why were the Cossacks cruel to the Jews?

4. Why did the girl keep her eyes closed?

5. Why didn't the whole family come to the United States together?

6. Why did the boat they were on arrive in New York?

7. Why couldn't they worship in Russia?

8. Why did Golda's parents think an education should be for a boy?

9. Why did the flag have the Star of David on it?

HAVE YOU EVER WONDERED?

1. How many world leaders are women?

2. Why were the Jews picked on?

3. Why do the Jews and Arabs not get along?

4. Where did the land for Israel come from?

5. How big is Israel?

6. Why is Jerusalem a holy city for many religions?

7. How have the people of Israel changed deserts into green fields?

8. What is the *Wailing Wall?*

WHAT IS YOUR OPINION?

1. Do you think young adults should always follow the advice of their parents? Why or why not?

SVETLANA ALLILUYEVA

The girl sat quietly.
She looked through the magazine.
Suddenly she stopped!
"No," she yelled, "This cannot be!"
"I don't believe it!"
What was in the magazine?

in the dark

The library
The library was crowded. No one spoke. Everyone was busily working. Some students wrote in their notebooks. Others looked at books on the shelves.

On the wall was a sign. It was written in Russian. It read, *Silence.*

One of the girls was very busy. She had many books in front of her. She wrote page after page. After a while, she stopped. The seventeen year old closed her book. She took a deep breath. "That was a lot of homework," she thought. "I'm glad I'm finished! Now I can relax."

The magazine section
Svetlana (*svet-LAH-nuh*) got up from her seat. It felt good to move around. She walked over to the magazine (*mag-uh-ZEEN*) section.

There were many magazines. They were from all parts of the world. Svetlana liked looking through them. It was nice to see how other people lived. It was fun looking at fashions.

Svetlana did not read the Russian magazines. She liked the foreign (*FAR-un*) ones. They gave her a chance to practice other languages.

Many languages
Svetlana knew many languages. She could speak Russian and German by the time she was six. English and other languages came later.

Svetlana took a magazine. It was one from America. She went back to her seat.

For a while the girl was quiet. She turned the pages. Then she stopped. There was a shriek (*SHREEK*)! The students around her looked up. "No," she yelled. "This cannot be! I don't believe it!"

"This cannot be!"

The magazine told of her mother's death. It was not the story she knew. The story spoke of suicide (*SOOW-uh-siyd*).

Her mother's death

Svetlana had been told her mother died naturally (*NAT-ruh-ly*). She believed this. Now, she learned otherwise. For ten years she was kept in the dark. For ten years she was told a lie.

The magazine taught her many things. The story also spoke of Joseph Stalin. He was her father.

Joseph Stalin

Joseph Stalin was the most powerful man in Russia. He ruled the country. Under him, millions of people suffered. He was cruel. No one could disobey him. He trusted very few people. Those he did not trust were killed or sent away. Everyone feared him. Millions hated him.

Svetlana's mother did not feel the same way. She felt sorry for the people. There was too much killing.

Svetlana's mother

There was too much suffering. She tried to tell this to her husband. She tried to change his thinking. It did not work. He would not listen.

Svetlana's parents

Svetlana's parents had not been happy. For thirteen years they argued and fought. Stalin came to hate his wife. He yelled at her. He insulted her. He threw things at her.

A big fight

Then one day there was a big fight. Stalin was very angry. He screamed and yelled. He would not leave his wife alone. This time, it was too much for the woman. She could not take it! She ran into her room crying. After a while, there was a shot. When the door was opened, she was on the floor. She had killed herself.

Svetlana was shocked

The magazine story shocked Svetlana. She began to wonder about many other things. "Was her father really so cruel? Why was her mother's death a mystery? Were other things being kept from her?"

Svetlana did not know what to believe. She was confused (*kun-FEWZD*).

Her childhood

Her thoughts went back to her childhood. They were happy days. There was much laughter and fun. She and her father had many happy times together. He was never too busy for her.

Vacation

Svetlana's happiest moments were in the summer. The warm weather meant fun. It meant swimming and horseback riding. It was vacation time!

The whole family spent its vacation together. Sometimes they went to their country house. It was outside of Moscow. Other times they went to the Black Sea. This was Stalin's favorite spot. It was his birthplace.

The Kremlin

Most of Svetlana's time was spent in the Kremlin. This was where the government buildings were located. This was where Stalin worked. Here Svetlana played.

Here she was protected (*pro-TEK-ted*).

Svetlana knew only beauty. There were pretty gardens. There were palaces and marble halls. Sorrow was kept from her. She could not see over the walls. She did not walk in the streets of Moscow. She could not hear the children begging.

Beauty and sorrow

When Svetlana was in her late teens things changed. Everywhere she went she was followed. Her telephone calls were listened to. Her private life was no longer her own.

Things changed

She learned the truth in the magazine. Her father could be a cruel person. His power was even used against her.

The truth

Stalin did not like Svetlana's boyfriend. The boy was sent away. He was not heard from for ten years.

Svetlana learned how heartless her father could be. Once she tried to speak on behalf of a friend's father. Svetlana asked Stalin to help the man. This made Stalin very angry. He yelled at his daughter. His answer was quick. He told her it was not her concern.

A heartless man

The young woman learned not to make close friends. It was useless. She saw too many of her friends suddenly leave. They never returned.

No close friends

Stalin died in 1953. Svetlana's life, however, did not change. The government still watched her. She was not free.

In 1963 she was told she could not marry the man she loved. The government gave no reason. The officials just said no.

The government

Three years later, the man became very ill. He wanted to return to his home in India. Svetlana was to go with him. The government said no again. A few months later he died.

Svetlana asked to go to India. She wanted to bring back the man's ashes. The government agreed.

In India, Svetlana made a decision. She would not return to Russia.

India

On April 21, 1967, Svetlana was a free woman. She arrived in the United States. She would never be in the dark again.

A free woman

ACTIVITIES

DID YOU GET THE MAIN IDEA? Svetlana came to the United States because:

a) she wanted to get married.

b) she wanted to be free.

c) she had ashes to bring.

d) her father sent her.

WHAT IS THE CORRECT ORDER?

1. Svetlana learns of her mother's suicide.

2. Svetlana's family vacations by the Black Sea.

3. Stalin dies.

4. Svetlana comes to the United States.

5. Svetlana goes to India.

6. Svetlana's mother dies.

IS IT RIGHT OR WRONG?

1. Svetlana was Stalin's daughter.

2. Svetlana's mother died a natural death.

3. Svetlana's parents were happily married.

4. The Kremlin is in India.

5. Svetlana had a happy childhood.

DO YOU REMEMBER?

1. The sign in the library was written in:

a) Russian.

b) German.

c) English.

2. Svetlana took one magazine. It came from:

   a) Russia.

   b) America.

   c) Germany.

3. By the time Svetlana was six she could speak:

   a) English and German.

   b) Russian and English.

   c) German and Russian.

4. The magazine said Svetlana's mother:

   a) died a natural death.

   b) committed suicide.

   c) was still alive.

5. Joseph Stalin was the most powerful man in:

   a) the United States.

   b) India.

   c) Russia.

6. Svetlana's parents were married for:

   a) ten years.

   b) thirteen years.

   c) three years.

7. Stalin's favorite vacation spot was:

   a) in Moscow.

   b) in India.

   c) on the Black Sea.

8. Svetlana's life began to change when:

   a) she was a child.

   b) she was in her late teens.

   c) her father died.

9. Stalin died in:

   a) 1967.

   b) 1963.

   c) 1953.

10. In 1967 Svetlana came to live in:

   a) the United States.

   b) Russia.

   c) Germany.

DO YOU KNOW THE MEANING?

1. "Joseph Stalin was the most <u>powerful</u> man in Russia." The opposite of powerful is:

   a) afraid.

   b) weak.

   c) strong.

2. "He <u>trusted</u> very few people." Trust means to:

   a) hate.

   b) think.

   c) believe.

3. "He <u>insulted</u> her." The opposite of insult is:

   a) yell.

   b) hate.

   c) praise.

4. "The magazine story <u>shocked</u> Svetlana." A shock is something:

   a) odd.

   b) known.

   c) not expected.

5. "This was Stalin's <u>favorite</u> spot." Favorite means to be liked:

   a) the best.

   b) the least.

   c) sometimes.

6. "Here she was <u>protected</u>." When someone protects you they:

   a) teach you.

   b) punish you.

   c) keep you safe.

7. "She could not hear the children <u>begging</u>." To beg means to:

   a) work for something.

   b) ask for something.

   c) give something away.

8. "Her <u>private</u> life was no longer her own." Private means:

   a) open.

   b) secret.

   c) public.

9. "He told her it was not her <u>concern</u>." Concern means to:

   a) like.

   b) leave alone.

   c) show interest.

10. "Svetlana made a <u>decision</u>." To decide means to:

   a) make up your mind.

   b) be confused.

   c) do nothing.

1. Why was there silence in the library?

2. Why did it feel good for Svetlana to move around?

3. Why was it fun to look at fashions?

4. Why did Svetlana learn many languages?

5. Why was the truth about her mother's death kept from Svetlana?

WHAT DO YOU THINK?

6. Why did Stalin let no one disobey him?

7. Why did the news in the magazine shock Svetlana?

8. Why was sorrow kept from Svetlana?

9. Why was Svetlana followed?

10. Why wouldn't Stalin listen to his daughter?

11. Why did the Russian government still watch Svetlana after Stalin's death?

12. Why did Svetlana decide to come to the United States?

HAVE YOU EVER WONDERED?

1. What are the major languages of the world?

2. How are Russian schools different from ours?

3. How many suicides are there in the United States each year?

4. What are some differences between Russia and the United States?

5. How did Stalin come to power?

6. What was the Kremlin once used for?

7. What do secret police do?

8. What is cremation?

9. What is done with people's ashes?

WHAT IS YOUR OPINION?

1. The truth about her mother's death was kept from Svetlana. Do you think it is always best to tell children the truth? Why or why not?

2. Do you think it is right for parents to interfere in their son's or daughter's romance? Explain your answer.

LAUREN BACALL

The producer needed an actress.
He saw a new face.
It was on the cover of a magazine.
Could he make that girl a star?

the big decision

The world of Hollywood The man gazed (*GAYZD*) out the window. He watched the scene below. It was all unreal. It was Hollywood.

The studio was a world of make believe. Everything and everyone was fake. Cowboys talked with ballerinas (*bahl-uh-REE-nuz*). Gangsters and Indians ate lunch together. There was action everywhere! Sheriffs and out-laws fought each other. Beautiful girls danced in Paris settings. Robbers fought with police.

The producer The man watching was a producer. He had worked on this lot for many years. He had seen many actors and actresses. Some made it to the top. They were the lucky ones. Thousands, however, never became stars. Many stayed in Hollywood anyway. They played bit parts in class *C* movies. They grew old hoping for the big break.

The producer stopped watching the scene. He walked away from the window. He began to mumble to himself. He could not help it. He was worried.

The producer had a big problem. It came from the head of the studio. He was told to make a big decision. He knew the danger in making the wrong choice. It could mean his job.

A big problem

The producer left the studio. He could not work. He headed home in his car. As he drove, he began to talk to himself. "Who should get the part?" he said. "Should it be the known star? Should I try my luck with an unknown? What should I do?" The decision had to be his own.

Who should it be?

When he got home he tried to relax. He could not. He paced up and down the room. He went over the choices many times.

At home

Finally, his wife told him to stop. "Listen honey," she said. "Stop worrying. You are very talented. You can make a star of anyone."

The producer's wife

As she spoke, she picked up a fashion magazine. She pointed to the girl on the cover. "Here," she said. "Why not make her a star!"

The producer listened. He picked up the magazine. The girl on the cover had a new, fresh face. It might work," he thought. "She's pretty all right! But, does she have talent?"

A new face

It did not take long to find out. A few telephone calls were made. Soon the pretty nineteen year old was in Hollywood.

The decision had been made. It proved to be the right one. Lauren Bacall (*LOR-en buh-KAWL*) was the girl on the magazine cover. She became one of Hollywood's biggest stars.

The decision

The name changes   Her real name was Betty Joan Perske (*PUR skee*). She did not keep this name. She and her mother used the name *Bacall*. It was her mother's maiden name. It was an English translation from a Rumanian name. Later, the name *Lauren* was used in place of Betty. Her new name became Lauren Bacall. It was the one she used on the stage and in the movies.

Few happy moments   The new star grew up in an unhappy home. Her parents did not get along. They were always fighting.

When Lauren was six, her parents were divorced. Lauren stayed with her mother. Once in a while her father came to see her. This did not last long. One day he said good-bye and never came back. It was the last time Lauren saw him.

Not kept down   Mother and daughter faced their problem. They were not going to let it keep them down. A way would be found to pay the rent. They would keep their two-room apartment.

Lauren's mother   Lauren's mother worked long hours. But she also made time for her daughter. She became both parents to her only child. The mother and daughter were drawn even closer together.

A dream   Lauren grew up with a dream. She wanted to be an actress. Her dream became her whole life.

Teen-age years   Her teen-age years were happy ones. They revolved around the Broadway stage. Her heroes were the people on the stage. She read about them. She collected pictures of them. She knew the lives of each of them.

Her heroes   Lauren worked after school as a model. She saved all the money she made. Every chance she had she went to the theater. She bought the cheapest seats. This way she could see many plays. She watched her heroes. These were some of the happiest moments of her life.

Lauren's only interest was the theater. Teachers *School* and school annoyed her. She cut class often. She went to Times Square. If there was a matinee (*mah-TIN-ay*), she was there.

Her teachers tried to make her study. They told her she would amount to nothing. Lauren did not care. She told anyone who wanted to listen. "Someday," she said, "I'm going to be a star."

She was right. Once in Hollywood things began to *Lauren marries* happen. Her first picture was with Humphrey Bogart. He was the top actor in Hollywood. Within the year they were married. She starred with him in many pictures. She became a success. Every producer wanted her.

The Bogart's lived a happy life. They spent twelve *Married life* years together. Then in 1957, it ended. Humphrey Bogart died of cancer. Once again a mother and her children were left alone. Lauren faced her problem. She decided it would not keep her down.

Lauren returned to her first love. She came back to *The comeback* Broadway. She wanted to make a comeback. She knew it would not be easy.

She did it! She was a success. Every show she was *The applause* in became a hit. The applause of Broadway was hers. *of New York*

The producer was right. Lauren proved that he had made the right decision.

ACTIVITIES

DID YOU GET THE MAIN IDEA?

Lauren Bacall proved the producer was right by:

a) marrying Humphrey Bogart.

b) becoming a star.

c) becoming a model.

d) changing her name.

WHAT IS THE CORRECT ORDER?

1. Humphrey Bogart dies.

2. Lauren's parents are divorced.

3. Lauren appears on a cover of a fashion magazine.

4. Lauren is called to Hollywood.

5. Lauren sees her father for the last time.

6. Lauren makes her comeback on Broadway.

IS IT RIGHT OR WRONG?

1. Stars play in class C movies.

2. Lauren was sixteen when she came to Hollywood.

3. Lauren's parents were divorced when she was six.

4. Lauren had a happy childhood.

5. Lauren and her mother lived in a four-room apartment.

DO YOU REMEMBER?

1. The producer watched the Hollywood scene from:

a) a car.

b) a window.

c) a stage.

2. The producer was afraid he might:

   a) lose his job.

   b) lose his wife.

   c) lose the studio.

3. The producer's wife picked up a:

   a) sports magazine.

   b) fashion magazine.

   c) garden magazine.

4. Lauren grew up in:

   a) Hollywood.

   b) New York.

   c) Rumania.

5. Lauren's real name was:

   a) Betty Joan Perske.

   b) Betty Bogart.

   c) Lauren Bacall.

6. Lauren's mother and father were:

   a) divorced.

   b) happy together.

   c) on the Broadway stage.

7. Lauren had:

   a) no brothers and sisters.

   b) one sister.

   c) one brother.

8. Humphrey Bogart was a famous:

   a) movie star.

   b) dancer.

   c) doctor.

9. Lauren made her comeback:

   a) on television.

   b) on Broadway.

   c) in the movies.

DO YOU KNOW THE MEANING?

1. "The man <u>gazed</u> out the window." To gaze means to look at something:

   a) for a long time.

   b) upside down.

   c) for a second.

2. "<u>Gangsters</u> and Indians ate lunch together." A gangster is a member of:

   a) the police force.

   b) a gang.

   c) a club.

3. "He began to <u>mumble</u> to himself." The opposite of mumble is to speak:

   a) loudly.

   b) quietly.

   c) clearly.

4. "He <u>paced</u> up and down the room." To pace means to:

   a) run.

   b) walk.

   c) hop.

5. "It was her mother's <u>maiden</u> name." A maiden is:

   a) an unmarried woman.

   b) a married woman.

   c) a divorced woman.

6. "She <u>collected</u> pictures of them." To collect means to:

   a) gather.

   b) give out.

   c) make.

7. "If there was a <u>matinee</u>, she was there." A matinee is a show held in:

   a) the afternoon.

   b) the evening.

   c) a tent.

8. "She wanted to make a <u>comeback</u>." A comeback is:

   a) a lot of money.

   b) a return.

   c) a new life.

9. "The <u>applause</u> of Broadway was hers." Applause is:

   a) cheers.

   b) fame.

   c) success.

WHAT DO YOU THINK?

1. Why is Hollywood a world of make believe?

2. Why are many pictures filmed at the same time?

3. Why don't many actors and actresses become stars?

4. Why might the wrong choice make the producer lose his job?

5. Why was Lauren's face on the cover of a magazine?

6. Why did Lauren and her mother change their names?

7. Why do actors and actresses have stage names?

8. Why did Lauren stay with her mother after the divorce?

9. Why didn't Lauren like school?

10. Why did Lauren become successful?

HAVE YOU EVER WONDERED?

1. How did Hollywood become the *movie capital of the world?*

2. What is it like to be a Hollywood star?

3. How long does it take to make a movie?

4. Why are many movies made outside the United States?

5. What are *extras?*

6. What does a *stunt man* do?

7. What is an *understudy?*

8. Why are critics important to Broadway shows?

9. How can a show fold in one night?

WHAT IS YOUR OPINION?

1. People say Hollywood stars make a lot of money. Do you think this is true? Do you think they should earn large salaries? Explain your answer.

2. Who is your favorite Hollywood star? What movies have you seen this person in? Why do you like this star?

HELEN DELICH BENTLEY

Helen was angry.
She walked up to the dockworker.
She pulled her arm back.
She punched him right on the jaw.
What made Helen so angry?

woman in a man's world

Hearty shouts Smoke filled the large room. The noise got louder. There were hearty (*HAR-tee*) shouts and much laughter. The waiters were kept busy. They ran back and forth from the kitchen. Each time, they brought a pitcher of beer.

The men were having a good time. Today was their day to relax. This was one day the ships could wait.

Longshoremen These men were a hardy bunch. They were used to the outdoors. They worked hard. Their bulging muscles (*MUS-ulz*) were proof of that. Their talk was rough (*RUF*) and to the point. There were no weaklings here. These were longshoremen (*LONG-shor-men*).

A man's world Here, the strong man was master. It was a place where actions, and not words, counted. It was a man's world except for one woman. Her name was Helen D. Bentley.

Mrs. Bentley Mrs. Bentley walked into the room. Some men con-
arrives tinued talking. Others stood and cheered. "Hi, Helen!" one man shouted. "Know any good jokes?"

Helen's nose Helen laughed and went on. Another man walked up to Helen. He was a little tipsy. "Hey, Helen," he yelled, "is your hair dyed? What happened to your nose? Is it still used as a ski slope?"

Helen was angry. She put her 130 pounds to use. She pulled her arm back. It moved fast. It landed on the dockworker's jaw.

On the jaw

Many of the men around her applauded. "That's showing him," they said. "I guess he won't bother you again."

Helen walked up to the stage. She began to speak. The men quieted down. They listened. Helen talked of things they knew. She talked about the sea.

Helen speaks

Helen's career (*ka-REER*) centered around the sea. Yet, her early life was very different.

Helen was born in the mountains of Nevada. She grew up in a copper-mining town. There was no water nearby. The ocean was hundreds of miles away.

Nevada

Helen's childhood was an unhappy one. Her two sisters and four brothers shared her sorrow. Their father was very sick. He was dying.

Sad childhood

Mr. Delich (*DEE-lik*) worked in a copper mine. Each day he went deep into the earth. For years he breathed the air in the tunnels. This air was killing him. It was filled with small pieces of dust. This dust filled his lungs. It made it hard for him to breathe.

The copper mine

Mr. Delich   The family tried to help. But it was no use. Mr. Delich was slowly dying. After a while, he got worse. The pains in his chest grew stronger. He began to cough more and more. He found it harder to breathe.

Mr. Delich grew very sick. He could work no more. He had to stay in bed. There was nothing anyone could do. There was no cure. Finally, when Helen was eight years old, he died.

Mrs. Delich   Mrs. Delich was alone. She had seven children to raise. She had a family to keep together.

Many years before, the Delichs had come from Yugoslavia (*YOU-gow-SLAV-ee-uh*). They came because of their children. They wanted them to get a good education.

Odd jobs   Mrs. Delich worked hard. She took in boarders. She did odd jobs. Helen also helped. When she was twelve years old she got a job. She worked in a dress shop. Their hard work paid off. None of the children had to leave school.

Helen's school days   Helen did not disappoint her mother. She did well in school. Her marks were high. She was president of her senior class. She was business manager of the yearbook. Helen enjoyed the social life of the school. The young girl took part in every club, dance, and event the school had to offer.

Graduation day   Helen's graduation day was an important event. Her mother was very proud of her. She received many awards and scholarships. She broke a record. No other student at White Pine High School had ever received more awards.

College   The scholarships were more than just awards. They were very important to Helen. They meant she could go to college.

Helen went to the Universities of Nevada and Missouri. She studied journalism (*JUR-nil-izm*). Once again, she did not disappoint her mother.

Hard work   Helen studied hard. She also had many jobs. Being a waitress and a drug-store clerk were some of them. Her work did not hurt her grades. She graduated college in three years.

After college, Helen became a reporter. She worked for the *Baltimore Sun*. She wrote many stories. They told of the problems of the waterfront. They made her famous. Helen, however, was not happy with just writing. She made her own television show. Here, she spoke of the importance of the shipping industry. "Our country," she said, "is in real trouble. Our merchant fleet is very old. In two or three years it will be too late. We will become a minor sea power. We will be in the hands of foreign powers."

A reporter

Not long after, Helen was called to Washington. The President asked for her help. He gave her a big job. She was made the head of the Federal Maritime Commission.

Washington

Helen's job was not an easy one. She had to handle many problems. Anything that had to do with the sea came under her control. She was always busy. The large ship lines had to be watched. Sometimes they tried to fix prices. If not checked, the smaller lines would be driven out of business. There was also a great deal of paper work.

No easy job

Helen had to make sure the ship companies carried insurance. In case of fire or damage, she made sure they were covered. Helen also handled oil spills. She found the company that caused the damage. Then, they were forced to clean the mess up. One of her most important jobs was the handling of labor problems. She helped end many strikes.

Helen did her job well. She won the respect of many people. On May 5, 1970, she was reappointed (*REE-uh-poyn-ted*) for a five-year term.

Today, as before, the shipping industry is still a man's world. The docks are still run by men. It's a private world, except for one woman. The exception (*ex-SEP-shun*) is Helen Delich Bentley. She is a woman in a man's world.

The exception

ACTIVITIES

Helen was the exception in a man's world because:

    a) her father died.

    b) she headed the Federal Maritime Commission.

    c) she came from Nevada.

    d) she was a reporter.

1. Helen works as a drug store clerk.

2. Mr. Delich dies.

3. Helen becomes the head of Federal Maritime Commission.

4. Helen graduates from White Pine High School.

5. Helen works in a dress shop.

6. Helen works for the *Baltimore Sun*.

1. Helen's parents came from Yugoslavia.

2. Helen had a happy childhood.

3. Helen hit the dockworker in the stomach.

4. Helen had a busy social life in high school.

5. Mr. Delich worked in a coal mine.

1. The longshoremen were:

    a) strong.

    b) weak.

    c) sad.

2. The longshoremen worked on:

    a) cars.

    b) ships.

    c) planes.

3. Helen was born near:

    a) the ocean.

    b) the mountains.

    c) the sea.

4. How many brothers did Helen have?

    a) two.

    b) four.

    c) seven.

5. Mr. Delich became sick:

    a) from breathing dust in a mine.

    b) from smoking too many cigarettes.

    c) after falling off a ship.

6. Mr. Delich died when Helen:

    a) was born.

    b) was eight years old.

    c) graduated from college.

7. The Delichs came to the United States so their children would have a better:

    a) home.

    b) job.

    c) education.

8. In college, Helen studied to be a:

    a) reporter.

    b) drug-store clerk.

    c) waitress.

158

9. Helen graduated from college in:
  a) three years.

  b) four years.

  c) five years.

10. Helen made her own:
  a) copper mine.

  b) newspaper.

  c) television show.

**DO YOU
KNOW THE
MEANING?**

1. "There were <u>hearty</u> shouts and much laughter."
Hearty means:
  a) nasty.

  b) old.

  c) friendly.

2. "Each time they brought a <u>pitcher</u> of beer." A pitcher
is a:
  a) glass.

  b) large container.

  c) painting.

3. "These men were a <u>hardy</u> bunch." Hardy means:
  a) strong.

  b) friendly.

  c) loud.

4. "Their <u>bulging</u> muscles were proof of that." Bulge
means to:
  a) be tired.

  b) be strong.

  c) stick out.

5. "There were no <u>weaklings</u> here." A weakling is a
person who is not:
  a) strong.

  b) old.

  c) rich.

6. "For years he breathed the air in the <u>tunnels</u>." A tunnel is:

   a) a cave.

   b) an underground passage.

   c) a road.

7. "She took in <u>boarders</u>." A boarder is someone who:

   a) lives in another person's house.

   b) lives in a hotel.

   c) has no money.

8. "Our merchant <u>fleet</u> is very old." A fleet is:

   a) a ship.

   b) a large group.

   c) a sailor.

9. "The <u>exception</u> is Helen Delich Bentley." An exception is something that is:

   a) different.

   b) the same.

   c) old.

1. Why were the waiters so busy?

2. Why were there no weaklings among the long-shoremen?

3. Why did actions count more than words?

4. Why did the men applaud Helen's punch to the jaw?

5. Why did Mr. Delich continue to work in the mine?

6. Why was there no cure for Mr. Delich?

7. Why did Helen join everything in school?

8. Why did Helen work while in college?

9. Why did Helen graduate college in three years?

10. Why wasn't Helen happy with just writing?

11. Why was Helen reappointed in 1970?

**HAVE YOU
EVER
WONDERED?**

1. How is copper ore mined?

2. What is *slurry*?

3. What are *anodes* and *cathodes*?

4. What are the properties of copper?

5. How does a ship stay afloat?

6. What is the world's largest ocean liner?

7. What is a *Merchant Marine Document*?

8. What are some of the international sea treaties?

9. What makes the *Savannah* different from other merchant ships?

**WHAT IS
YOUR OPINION?**

1. What problems does a woman in a man's world have? Why do you think most men respect Helen?

2. What do you think would be interesting about a career in journalism? What do you think would be difficult about such a career?

ANDY BATHGATE

The dressing room door opened.
A husky Ranger player came out.
"Which of you guys wants a stick?" he said.
Andy was lucky! He got one!
How did he later show his thanks?

a boy remembers

Before the game For a second there was silence. A man in a striped shirt skated around. He was the referee (*ref-uh-REE*). He examined the rink. It took a while. The rink was two hundred feet long. Some other men watched. They wore padded suits. These men were rugged looking. They held their curved wooden sticks tightly.

Excitement The calm did not remain for long. The excitement began at once. The referee dropped a round piece of hard rubber called a puck. It fell to the ice.

The puck was loose Chips of ice flew in the air. The puck was loose. Two men raced for it. They tried to hit it with their sticks. One of them did! It moved at a speed of ninety miles an hour. It was passed back and forth. It moved up and down the ice.

Five skaters from each side chased it. They flashed up and down the rink. They tried to get control of the puck.

Each player looked at the end of the rink. They eyed the other team's net. A goalkeeper (*GOWL-keep-ur*) stood in front of the net. He looked mean. His job was a hard one. He had to stop the puck from going into the net. Sometimes he could not. This meant a point for the other team.

The game was being watched by a bunch of wide-eyed Canadian boys. They came each day. They watched the Rangers practice.

The Rangers

The Rangers were a New York hockey team. They trained in Winnepeg, Canada before each season.

Young Andy Bathgate was one of the young boys. He watched each player. He studied them. His eyes took in everything. Every move and play had a meaning. He knew he had a lot to learn.

One of the onlookers

The boys waited for the game to end. When it did, they followed the players. They walked and chatted with them. They stopped at the entrance to the dressing room. The players went inside.

The players

Sometimes the boys were lucky. They got a used stick. It was one that was cracked in the game.

The boys were careful. They turned their heads every so often. They had to look for the guard. He did not like them. He often chased them away.

The guard

"He's not here today," one of the boys shouted.

"We're safe," another boy laughed. "Maybe the old guy fell. He can't get up because his weight is keeping him down." The boys felt relaxed. They all joined in the laughter.

"Maybe I'll be lucky today," Andy thought. "Maybe I'll get a stick. I hope it's just a little cracked. I could sure use one."

Andy's hopes

The dressing room door opened. A husky (*HUS-key*) Ranger player came out. He looked at the boys. They were all around him.

The dressing room door

The boys were in luck! Many sticks were cracked that day.

"All right," he said. "Which of you guys wants a stick?" All the boys shouted. They raised their hands.

Andy was lucky. He got one of the good sticks. He was happy. He headed for home. "Boy," he thought, "just a little tape around the edge will do it. This stick will be like new. I can't wait to try it out. It sure feels great!"

A good stick

Andy loved hockey. He got up at four in the morning. He walked five miles to the Rangers' camp. He was tired.

Hockey

But he didn't mind. It was worth it. He got a stick that day!

Hockey was a part of Andy's life. When he got home, he practiced. He tried the plays he saw that day. Over and over, he tried the new shots. When it grew dark, he came inside. He read hockey magazines. He even kept a scrap book. At night, he listened to hockey games. A radio was always near his bed. Sometimes he fell asleep listening to the game.

Andy learned hockey at an early age. His brother and sister were his teachers. His sister taught him to skate as soon as he was able to stand. His brother helped too. When Andy was six, his brother gave him a hockey stick. A year later, he was playing.

Mr. Bathgate's Scottish temper was often aroused (*uh-ROWZD*). At times he wished his youngest son had a different sport. Hockey could be expensive. Andy's sport was costing Mr. Bathgate money.

It took awhile for Andy to learn. He practiced daily. Sometimes his shots went astray. The puck did not end up in the net. It went flying through the air instead. Sometimes it crashed through a window. This angered Andy's father even more.

Mr. Bathgate did not stay angry for long. There were not many windows broken. Andy learned quickly. When he was twelve, he played on six different teams. He even coached another team.

In 1949, Andy surprised many people. By now he was a good player. Many clubs wanted him. Some of the leading Canadian clubs tried to get him. To play for such a team meant instant (*IN-stent*) success. Fame and glory would be his.

Andy refused. Instead he chose a New York club. He signed with the Rangers. Later, he was asked why. People did not understand his move. Andy told them the story of his childhood. He told them of the Ranger who once gave him a stick.

Andy Bathgate did not forget. He remembered the good deed. He paid it back.

ACTIVITIES

Andy showed he remembered by:

a) getting a stick.

b) playing hockey.

c) signing with the Rangers.

d) getting up at four.

DID YOU
GET THE
MAIN IDEA?

1. Andy gets a broken stick.

2. Andy gets a hockey stick from his brother.

3. Andy's sister teaches him to skate.

4. Andy coaches a hockey team.

5. Andy signs with the Rangers.

6. Andy watches the Rangers train.

WHAT IS
THE CORRECT
ORDER?

1. A puck in a net means one point.

2. The Rangers are a Canadian team.

3. Andy's first stick came from his sister.

4. The guard often chased the boys.

5. Mr. Bathgate was Scottish.

IS IT
RIGHT OR
WRONG?

1. A round piece of hard rubber is a:

a) puck.

b) stick.

c) skate.

DO YOU
REMEMBER?

2. How many men are on a hockey team?

   a) five.

   b) six.

   c) seven.

3. The group watching the practice games were:

   a) girls.

   b) Rangers.

   c) boys.

4. The Rangers trained in:

   a) New York.

   b) Winnepeg.

   c) Buffalo.

5. Sometimes the boys got a:

   a) puck.

   b) stick.

   c) skate.

6. Who sometimes chased the boys?

   a) the referee.

   b) a Ranger player.

   c) the guard.

7. Andy made his stick like new by:

   a) putting glue on it.

   b) taping it.

   c) nailing it.

8. How far was the Ranger camp from Andy's home?

   a) four miles.

   b) five miles.

   c) two miles.

9. Andy sometimes broke:

    a) dishes.

    b) windows.

    c) sticks.

10. When Andy was twelve, how many teams was he on?

    a) one.

    b) six.

    c) three.

1. "A man in a striped shirt skated around." A stripe is:

   a) round.

   b) square.

   c) narrow.

2. "He was the referee." A referee is a:

   a) coach.

   b) player.

   c) judge.

3. "Chips of ice flew in the air." A chip is something:

   a) large.

   b) small.

   c) round.

4. "They flashed up and down the rink." To flash means to move:

   a) quickly.

   b) slowly.

   c) calmly.

5. "They walked and chatted with them." Chat means to:

   a) move.

   b) talk.

   c) listen.

6. "The boys felt relaxed." The opposite of relaxed is:

   a) nervous.

   b) calm.

   c) noisy.

7. "Just a little tape around the edge will do it." The edge is the:

   a) middle.

   b) side.

   c) bottom.

8. "Sometimes his shots went <u>astray</u>." The opposite of astray is:

   a) wander.

   b) move about.

   c) stay in one place.

9. "He even <u>coached</u> another team." A coach is a:

   a) player.

   b) teacher.

   c) referee.

WHAT DO
YOU THINK?

1. Why did the referee examine the rink?

2. Why did the players wear padded suits?

3. Why did the boys come to watch the practice games?

4. Why did the team practice in Canada?

5. Why didn't the boys go into the dressing room?

6. Why did the guard chase the boys?

7. Why didn't the players keep cracked sticks?

8. Why do boys in Canada play hockey?

9. Why did Andy's shots go astray at first?

10. Why would being on a Canadian team mean instant success?

HAVE YOU EVER WONDERED?

1. Why is hockey the national sport of Canada?

2. Is hockey only played on ice?

3. What does *icing the puck* mean?

4. What is the penalty box?

5. What is a power play?

6. How much does a goalkeeper's equipment weigh?

7. What is the Stanley Cup?

8. Why is hockey one of the roughest sports?

WHAT IS YOUR OPINION?

1. Describe a good deed which someone did for you. Did you pay back the person in any way? If you did, explain how? If you did not, what can you do now to pay back the favor?

2. Have you ever had to make a difficult choice? What did the choice involve? What helped you to make up your mind? Do you think you made the correct choice?

ANDY WARHOL

The telephone rang.
Andy went to answer it.
"No, don't shoot!" he yelled.
She did not listen.
She fired her gun.
Was Andy killed?

the mystery man

A Monday in June It was a Monday in June. The year was 1968. The place was a studio in New York City.

A man and woman rode up the elevator (*EL-uh-vay-tor*). When they reached the sixth floor, they got off. The two entered the studio, or *Factory*, as it was called. The man was Andy Warhol. The woman was an unknown actress.

Andy's world The *Factory* was Andy's world. Here he created (*kree-AY-ted*). Here his famous Pop Art was produced.

A strange place The *Factory* was a strange place. Everything seemed real, yet unreal. The walls were like mirrors. They were covered with silver foil (*FOYL*). Everything in the room appeared larger than it was.

Common things The studio was filled with common things. There were things one sees every day. Yet, somehow, they seemed different. Giant rolls of paper hung from the ceiling. Big, bright flowers were printed on each. Giant Coke bottles stood in one corner. Hundreds of wooden boxes were piled in the center of the room. They were brightly colored. The name on each was familiar. On each box, letters spelled the word *Brillo*. Against the wall was a moving belt. On it were more boxes. Soon, they too would become one of Andy's works of art.

Andy inspected the dyes. He checked the colors. *Printing the boxes* The silk screen was working right. Then, he and two other men went to work. The actress sat and rested. She watched as the men began to paint the boxes.

While they were working, the telephone rang. Andy went to answer it.

While Andy talked, the actress moved to the center *The gun* of the room. No one noticed as she opened her pocketbook. Her hand fumbled inside for a minute. Then she found what she was looking for. It was a gun. She aimed it at Andy.

Andy spotted the gun. He looked into the eyes of the actress. "No, don't shoot!" he yelled. "Don't kill me!"

The woman did not listen. She pulled the trigger. *Shots* Three shots were fired.

One of the bullets hit Andy. He fell to the floor. He kept repeating, "It hurts! It hurts!" The woman was disarmed. Andy was taken to a hospital.

The hospital

Soon a large crowd gathered. Reporters and cameramen (*KAM-ruh-men*) were everywhere. They waited for the news. "Is he going to live?" asked one of the men. "How bad is he?" asked another.

The doctor

One doctor tried to answer their questions. "The bullet has caused (KAWZD) much damage," the doctor said. He is being operated on right now. His chances are not too good. It will be a while before we know more."

Andy's mother

Andy's mother came to the hospital. She listened to the doctors. She asked to see her son. "I'm sorry," the doctor said. "Your son is still in the operating room. You'll have to wait."

The mystery man

Mrs. Warhol tried to leave. It was too late! The reporters saw her. They asked her many questions. Would she tell them something about her son? They knew very little about him. He was a *mystery man*.

The reporters learned little. Andy always lived in the present. The past for him had no meaning. Tomorrow he left for the future.

However, Andy did have a past. He was born and *Andy's past*
raised in Pennsylvania. He was the son of Czechoslo-
vakian immigrants. Eight years before his birth, his
parents came to the United States.

From the start, art was the center of Andy's life. It *Art in his life*
was the one thing he really enjoyed. As a child, he often
cut up pictures. From these, he made his own drawings.
All through school, art was his best subject. In college,
he majored in art. He studied to be a commercial (*kum-
MER-shul*) artist.

When Andy was in his early twenties he came to *New York*
New York. He got a job as an illustrator (*IL-lus-tray-tur*).
Andy also decorated store windows. His window displays
made him famous. In one store, he put blow-ups of comic
strip characters. Not long thereafter, he became world
famous.

Andy became the leader in the Pop Art field. This *Pop Art leader*
man brought something new to art. He made blow-ups of
money and movie stars. They were talked about everywhere. He drew large pictures of typewriters and telephones. His pictures brought a freshness to the art world.
A picture of a Campbell's soup can was his most famous
work. Later, this picture sold for $60,000.

Not everyone liked the young man's paintings. Andy *Not always*
did not care. He was happy in what he was doing. After *liked*
all, his works were a part of today's machine age. He
argued with his critics (*KRIT-iks*) about his soup painting.
"They accept a picture of a bowl of fruit as art," he said.
"Yet they will not accept my picture. What is wrong with
a can of soup? Why is one accepted and the other not?"

Andy had been asked why he chose to paint such *Why he painted*
things. His answer was a simple one. "I paint things I like,"
he said. "I like soup. Money, of course, I always liked. It
was something I never had enough of."

Now, however, money was not important. Andy was
in the operating room. He was fighting for his life.

After five hours, the doctor came out. Everyone *The operation*
waited for his words. "Andy Warhol is alive," he said. *was over*
"He will live to see tomorrow!"

ACTIVITIES

DID YOU GET THE MAIN IDEA?

The reporters called Andy a mystery man because:

a) he was shot.

b) he painted common things.

c) they knew very little about him.

d) he worked in the *Factory*.

WHAT IS THE CORRECT ORDER?

1. Andy is shot.

2. The operation is over.

3. Andy's mother comes to the hospital.

4. Andy is taken to the hospital.

5. The actress fumbles in her pocketbook.

6. Andy and the actress enter the *Factory*.

IS IT RIGHT OR WRONG?

1. Andy's parents were born in Pennsylvania.

2. Andy had two brothers.

3. Andy's best subject was science.

4. When Andy was in his teens he came to New York.

5. Andy was shot three times.

DO YOU REMEMBER?

1. Andy's studio is in:

a) Czechoslovakia.

b) Pennsylvania.

c) New York.

2. Andy's studio is called:
   a) the *Factory*.

   b) Carnegie Tech.

   c) Pop Art.

3. The walls in the studio were covered with:
   a) paint.

   b) wall paper.

   c) silver foil.

4. Andy was shot by a (an):
   a) reporter.

   b) cameraman.

   c) actress.

5. In school, Andy studied to be a:
   a) teacher.

   b) commercial artist.

   c) doctor.

6. What picture sold for $60,000?
   a) his typewriter.

   b) his movie star.

   c) his Campbell's soup can.

7. Andy painted common things because:
   a) it was easy.

   b) he liked them.

   c) it was all he knew.

8. Mrs. Warhol told the reporters:
   a) Andy's life story.

   b) very little.

   c) nothing.

9. Andy's operation took:
   a) one hour.

   b) five hours.

   c) ten hours.

178

1. "The place was a studio in New York City." A studio is a:

   a) kitchen.

   b) workroom.

   c) living room.

2. "Here he created." The opposite of create is to:

   a) make.

   b) destroy.

   c) put together.

3. "Hundreds of boxes were piled in the center of the room." Things piled are:

   a) on top of each other.

   b) broken.

   c) scattered all about.

4. "Andy inspected the boxes." To inspect means to:

   a) leave alone.

   b) pass over.

   c) look at.

5. "She <u>aimed</u> it at Andy." To aim is to:

  a) point.

  b) miss.

  c) drop.

6. "Tomorrow, he left for the <u>future</u>." The opposite of the future is:

  a) tomorrow.

  b) the present.

  c) the past.

7. "Here, he studied to be a <u>commercial</u> artist." Commercial has to do with:

  a) a religion.

  b) business.

  c) education.

8. "His window <u>displays</u> made him famous." To display is to:

  a) hide.

  b) show.

  c) leave alone.

9. "He drew large pictures of <u>typewriters</u> and telephones." A typewriter is used to make:

  a) words.

  b) music.

  c) pictures.

10. "He argued with his <u>critics</u>." A critic is one who makes:

  a) a play.

  b) a judgment.

  c) a book.

1. Why was the studio called the *Factory?*

2. Why did things in the *Factory* seem unreal?

3. Why did no one notice the actress?

4. Why did the actress fumble in her pocketbook?

5. Why did a large crowd gather at the hospital?

6. Why did the doctor say his chances are not too good?

7. Why wouldn't the doctor let Andy's mother see him?

8. Why did Andy keep his early life a mystery?

9. Why did Andy's parents leave Czechoslovakia?

10. Why did Andy major in art?

11. Why did Andy come to New York?

12. Why were Andy's pictures talked about everywhere?

1. What is Pop Art?

2. Why is it called Pop Art?

3. Who are some of the other famous "Pop" artists?

4. Where is Czechoslovakia?

5. What does the word *Czechoslovakia* mean?

6. What makes a bullet leave a gun?

7. What happens to a bullet when it enters a person?

8. How is a bullet taken out of a person?

9. Why are most people not awake during an operation?

1. Have you ever seen a photo or a painting that you liked? Why did you like it?

2. There are other kinds of artists besides painters. For example, sculptors, writers, musicians, actors, and architects are also artists. Which kind of art interests you the most? Why?

WELTHY FISHER

The ringleader stood up.
She picked up her bowl of rice.
"I'm not going to eat this slop!" she said.
With that, she threw the bowl on the floor.
How did Miss Welthy handle this problem?

welthy teaches millions

School of the Protecting Spirit

All seemed peaceful at the School of the Protecting Spirit. The girls were in their classes. They were busily studying.

The sun went down

Outside, the sun was slowly going down. Its light was everywhere. It covered the hills of Nanchang, China. It hit the roof of the school. Everything turned a golden yellow. Then, in an instant, it grew dark. The sun had disappeared. For fifty girls another school day ended.

The girls left their classes. Some walked outside. Others returned to their rooms.

An evil plan

The quiet was misleading (*mis-LEE-ding*). All was not peaceful. Something evil was being planned.

A small group of girls began to gather. They met behind the main building. They were in a nasty mood. The leader spoke. "Who does that teacher think she is?" she said. "Why should we have to take orders from her? We'll show our principal we don't want that teacher here."

A wicked smile came over the girl's face. "We'll make things very hard for her!" she said.

The next day the girls made their move. It was at mealtime. The ringleader stood up. She waited until all eyes were on her. Then she picked up her bowl of rice. "I'm not going to eat this slop!" she yelled. With that, she threw the bowl on the floor.

The girls make their move

The girl's eyes looked straight at the teacher. She walked up to her. "And no one here is going to make me," the leader yelled.

The rest of the girls waited. They watched to see what would happen.

The rest waited

The teacher stood still. She did not yell. She did nothing.

The girls were no longer afraid. They saw their leader was not being punished. They joined in.

The lunchroom was a mess. Rice flew through the air. Empty bowls covered the floor.

The lunchroom

The ringleader smiled at her friends. "I guess we'll see some changes around here," she said. "Maybe now we'll be treated better. Maybe now Miss Welthy will get rid of her."

The head of the school came into the room. She walked over to the teacher. She looked at the mess on the floor. Then the principal looked at the girls.

The head of the school

Miss Welthy spoke in a loud, clear voice. "This teacher is in charge here. Soon, she will be the head of this school. If you cannot listen to her, you cannot stay. Either obey or leave."

Obey or leave

The girls did not believe Miss Welthy. "How could she keep her word?" they thought. "Didn't she need them? Didn't their parents pay for the school? Surely they would make her do as they wanted."

The girls wait

The girls walked out of the room. They went to their rooms. They waited to be called back. The call never came.

She kept her word

The girls found that Miss Welthy kept her word. Their American principal was not afraid. She showed everyone. She did not give in. She did what she thought was right.

A life of surprises

Mrs. Welthy Fisher's life was full of surprises. She always did the unexpected. Her decisions surprised many people. Yet, she stood by each.

Her childhood

Mrs. Fisher's early life was not unusual. It gave no clue (*KLOO*) to her future. The Dutch-American was born Welthy Honsinger. She grew up in a big house in Rome, New York.

Welthy's childhood was a happy one. Her house was always full of laughter and games. There was always someone to play with. Welthy had two sisters and a brother. She also had four half brothers and a half sister.

A beautiful voice

Everyone thought Welthy would someday be an opera (*OP-ruh*) singer. She had a beautiful voice. Her parents sent her to a special school. There she learned many things. She did special exercises. She trained her voice. In a short time, her voice grew stronger. It improved. She was on her way to becoming an opera star.

The music lessons were expensive. A way had to be found to pay for them. Welthy found a way. After college, she became a teacher. In the daytime she taught. She went to music school in the evening.

A teacher

One evening, Welthy went to a lecture (*LEK-chur*). It changed her life. The speaker was a missionary (*MISH-uh-ner-ee*). He spoke of far-away places. He spoke of the people who needed help.

The lecture

Welthy made up her mind. She would become a missionary. She wanted to go to China. Nothing would stop her.

Welthy's whole life changed. She left behind her musical career. She gave up her plans for marriage. She left her relatives (*REL-uh-tivz*) and friends.

What she left

The years that followed were busy ones. In China, she helped change many old ideas. She opened her school to all. Orphans (*OR-fenz*) and poor children were welcome. She added many new subjects. Music and science were taught. She fought against many old customs. In her school, white and Chinese girls lived together.

China

In 1924, Welthy married Frederick Fisher. He was also a missionary. He was bishop of India and Burma. They lived in Calcutta, India for a while. Later, they moved to Ann Arbor, Michigan.

Marriage

After her husband's death, Welthy returned to India. She came to keep a promise. Before Mohandas Gandhi (*GON-dee*) died, he asked Welthy to help the people of India. He wanted her to teach his people to read and write.

India

Welthy worked to make Gandhi's dream come true. She began with a one-room school house. She named the school *"Literacy (LIT-er-uh-see) House."* Here she taught others to teach. Her teachers went into the villages of India. They traveled by bicycle. They took their school with them. They used roll-up blackboards. They brought puppets. They used books Mrs. Fisher wrote.

Literacy House

After fifteen years, Gandhi's dream came true. Ten thousand teachers had been taught. Two million people had been taught to read and write. Mrs. Welthy Fisher had done her job well.

A dream come true

ACTIVITIES

DID YOU GET THE MAIN IDEA? Miss Welthy handled the ringleader at school by:

a) cleaning up the lunchroom.

b) not giving in.

c) teaching music and science.

d) throwing rice.

WHAT IS THE CORRECT ORDER?

1. Miss Welthy gets married.

2. *Literacy House* begins.

3. Miss Welthy becomes a teacher.

4. Miss Welthy goes to college.

5. Mr. Fisher dies.

6. Miss Welthy goes to China.

IS IT RIGHT OR WRONG?

1. The School of the Protecting Spirit was in China.

2. Mohandas Gandhi was a Chinese leader.

3. Welthy became a missionary.

4. The girls cleaned up the lunchroom.

5. Welthy became an opera singer.

DO YOU REMEMBER?

1. The school day ended when:

a) the sun came up.

b) the sun went down.

c) the bell rang.

2. How many girls were in the School of the Protecting Spirit?

    a) 50.

    b) 100.

    c) 150.

3. The girls made their move in the:

    a) courtyard.

    b) classroom.

    c) lunchroom.

4. Welthy Fisher grew up in:

    a) India.

    b) China.

    c) the United States.

5. Everyone thought Welthy would become a (an):

    a) missionary.

    b) opera singer.

    c) teacher.

6. To make money, Welthy became a:

    a) teacher.

    b) opera singer.

    c) missionary.

7. Miss Welthy married a:

    a) singer.

    b) bishop.

    c) leader.

8. Gandhi wanted Welthy to teach his people to:

    a) farm.

    b) sing.

    c) read and write.

9. Mrs. Fisher's teachers traveled by:

   a) car.

   b) bicycle.

   c) plane.

DO YOU KNOW THE MEANING?

1. "Something <u>evil</u> was being planned." The opposite of evil is:

   a) good.

   b) bad.

   c) mean.

2. "They were in a <u>nasty</u> mood." Nasty means to be:

   a) happy.

   b) sad.

   c) unpleasant.

3. "A <u>wicked</u> smile came over the girl's face." Wicked means to be:

   a) bad.

   b) good.

   c) silly.

4. "I'm not going to eat this <u>slop</u>." Slop is food that is:

   a) tasty.

   b) not tasty.

   c) stale.

5. "It gave no <u>clue</u> to her future." A clue is a:

   a) story.

   b) hint.

   c) problem.

6. "One evening Welthy went to a <u>lecture</u>." A lecture is a:

   a) dance.

   b) speech.

   c) party.

7. "The speaker was a <u>missionary</u>." A missionary works for a:

   a) government.

   b) music school.

   c) church.

8. "She left her <u>relatives</u> and friends." Relatives are people in the same:

   a) school.

   b) family.

   c) city.

9. "<u>Orphans</u> and poor children were welcome." An orphan has no:

   a) parents.

   b) sisters and brothers.

   c) money.

1. How did the sun turn everything a golden yellow?

2. Why did the girls meet in secret?

3. Why did the ringleader wait until all eyes were on her?

4. Why did the other girls wait before they joined in?

5. Why did the ringleader think there would be changes made?

6. Why didn't the girls believe Miss Welthy?

7. Why did Welthy go to a special music school?

8. How did Welthy's life change after she left the United States?

9. Why did Gandhi want his people to read and write?

10. Why did Welthy call her school *Literacy House?*

1. Why are missionaries sometimes killed?

2. Why do Chinese people eat with chopsticks?

3. Why is rice always a part of a Chinese meal?

4. What is a half sister?

5. What is an opera?

6. What is a bishop?

7. What did Gandhi do for India?

8. How did Gandhi die?

1. What do you think would be most difficult about being a missionary? What do you think would be most rewarding?

2. Have you or someone you know ever "tested" a teacher? Describe what happened. What did the teacher do?

BARONESS MARIA VON TRAPP

They were about to go inside.
They stopped to listen.
It sounded like church bells.
All the churches were ringing their bells.
Why were the bells a reason for sorrow?

the story of the bells

Agatha's birthday Maria and Georg Trapp smiled at each other. They sat down for their evening meal. Their nine children ate quickly. The parents knew why. It was March 11, 1938. It was a special day. It was Agatha's birthday. Her brothers and sisters could not wait. They were excited. They wanted to begin the party. They wanted to give her the presents they made.

The family finished eating. They got ready to go into the living room. The presents and the cake were waiting.

"Come, children!" said Mr. Trapp. Come here. Look at what is happening."

The last rays of sunlight The family went outside. It was a beautiful evening. The sun was going down. The last rays of sunlight brought many changes. The color of the hills changed. They turned a reddish gray. Spring flowers began to close. Everything seemed peaceful.

Georg put his arm around Maria. They smiled. God had been good to them.

They stopped to listen They were about to go inside. They stopped for a second. What was the sound? They listened. It sounded like church bells. The ringing of the bells grew louder. They came from afar. They came from the city of Salzburg.

The family looked at each other. They were puzzled. What could be happening? What was the happy event? What caused the ringing of the bells?

The ringing of bells

They went inside. Mr. Trapp went to the telephone. He tried to find out what was happening. All the lines were busy. "Father," said one of the children. "Why not put the radio on."

The family gathered around the radio. They listened. A voice shouted, "Austria (*AWS-tree-uh*) is no more. Austria is now a part of Germany! Listen as the people of Salzburg greet us. Listen to the church bells. Hear the joy that is here! Listen how we are loved!"

Austria is no more

The Trapp family was not happy. They could not believe their ears. They did not share in this joy. Tears filled their eyes. "We cannot believe this," they said. "How could this happen? Austria will never die. It will stay alive in our hearts!"

In April, Maria went to Salzburg. She rode her bicycle. It was no longer a happy town. It had turned into a jail. Flags were everywhere. They were red and black. They were Nazi (*NAT-zee*) flags. Everything and everyone seemed different. People were afraid. No one spoke. No one could be trusted or believed.

The city changed

Maria found a person she could trust. It was her parish (*PAR-ish*) priest (*PREEST*). He told her of many changes. The Nazis took over everything. They changed the laws. You could not disobey. Those who did were taken away. They were never heard from again.

The Nazis

The old priest told her more. The schools had changed. Children were told there was no god. They were told not to believe their parents.

There was something else Maria learned. She learned the true story of the bells. "The world has been misled," the priest said. "They think we welcomed the Nazis. It is not true! The world heard the radio broadcast (*BRAWD-kast*). They heard the bells of our churches ringing. We did not want to ring the bells. We were made to do it. Nazi soldiers stood behind us with guns. They made us ring the bells."

The world was misled

Maria went home. She told Georg the sad news. They made up their minds. Austria was not safe. They could not stay. They would have to escape.

Escape

Maria and her family fled. They went over the mountains into Italy. They were just in time. The border was closed the next day.

The Trapp family left much in Austria. They no longer had wealth. They had to leave their money. They left their house and servants.

But the family was together and free. That is what counted. They were happy.

A job is offered

The Trapp family was offered a job. They were asked to sing in the United States. They quickly took the job. They took the first boat to New York.

New York

New York was different. It was nothing like Salzburg. There were tall buildings and subways. There was a new language and the customs were different. It was all strange at first.

The family did well. People liked to hear their songs. They visited forty-eight states. They learned a lot. Their new land became their home.

A new home

In 1942, the Trapp family bought a farm. It was in Vermont. They built a new home. It was much like the one they had left in Austria.

The old army camp

Later, they took over an old army camp. This was Maria's idea. She wanted to make others happy. They turned the camp into a resort (*ree-ZORT*). People came there in the summer. They came for their vacations. They sang and lived outdoors. People had fun.

An interesting life

Maria's life was interesting. Her life was made into a Broadway play. Later it was made into a movie. The name was *The Sound of Music*. Her story was told to millions. The picture was a big success. It was one of the best ever. Maria made money from the picture.

The chapel

The money was spent wisely. The family put up a chapel (*CHAP-pul*). It was built on their land. Soon there was the sound of bells. They rang throughout the Vermont hills. But now the bells were telling a new story.

ACTIVITIES

The bells were ringing in Salzburg because:

DID YOU GET THE MAIN IDEA?

- **a)** the people were happy.
- **b)** it was a beautiful evening.
- **c)** it was Sunday.
- **d)** the priests were forced to ring them.

WHAT IS THE CORRECT ORDER?

1. Salzburg is turned into a jail.
2. The church bells ring in Salzburg.
3. The priest talks to Maria.
4. The family listens to the radio.
5. The family escapes to Italy.
6. The family builds a new home in Vermont.

IS IT RIGHT OR WRONG?

1. The Trapp children bought their sister birthday presents.
2. Germany took over Austria.
3. The Nazis changed the laws.
4. The members of the Trapp family were singers.
5. People came to the family's resort in the winter.

DO YOU REMEMBER?

1. March 11 was:
   - **a)** Maria's birthday.
   - **b)** Georg's birthday.
   - **c)** Agatha's birthday.

2. The family went outside to watch:
   a) the sun go down.

   b) the flowers open.

   c) the Austrian mountains.

3. The sound of church bells was coming from:
   a) Salzburg.

   b) Germany.

   c) Italy.

4. The family gathered around:
   a) the telephone.

   b) the radio.

   c) the church.

5. The Nazis were:
   a) Austrians.

   b) Germans.

   c) Americans.

6. Maria heard the truth about the bells from:
   a) Agatha.

   b) Georg.

   c) a priest.

7. People who disobeyed the Nazis were:
   a) taken away.

   b) rewarded.

   c) left alone.

8. The Trapp family escaped to:
   a) Germany.

   b) Italy.

   c) the United States.

9. In 1942, the Trapp family bought:
   a) a farm.

   b) an army camp.

   c) a resort.

10. *The Sound of Music* was:

   a) a television show.

   b) a movie.

   c) a book.

1. "They were puzzled." Puzzled means to be:

   a) torn apart.

   b) confused.

   c) worried.

DO YOU KNOW THE MEANING?

2. "What was the happy event?" An event is:

   a) a birthday.

   b) a party.

   c) something that happens.

3. "It was her parish priest." A parish is:

   a) a church.

   b) a church district.

   c) a poor area.

4. "The world had been misled." To mislead means to:

   a) fool.

   b) tell the truth.

   c) hide.

5. "They would have to escape." To escape is to:

   a) go away.

   b) stay.

   c) hide.

6. "The border was closed the next day." A border is:

   a) a mountain pass.

   b) the edge of a country.

   c) a hotel.

7. "They turned the camp into a resort." A resort is a:

   a) shopping center.

   b) park.

   c) vacation spot.

8. "The family put up a <u>chapel</u>." A chapel is a:
   a) music room.
   b) place of worship.
   c) monument.

WHAT DO YOU THINK?

1. Why did Maria and Georg think God had been good to them?

2. Why did the Nazis want the church bells rung?

3. Why were the telephone lines busy?

4. Why were there tears in the eyes of the Trapp family?

5. Why could no one be trusted or believed in Salzburg?

6. Why did the family want to escape?

7. Why did the family take the job in the United States?

8. Why did they build a home like the one they had in Austria?

9. Why did they build a chapel?

HAVE YOU EVER WONDERED?

1. How does the sun change the color of the hills?

2. Why do churches have bells?

3. Why do countries have flags?

4. Why did the Nazis tell the children there was no God?

5. How do countries protect their borders?

6. Why are there many tall buildings in New York City?

7. How much money does a person get for having his life made into a movie?

8. How is a chapel different from a church?

WHAT IS YOUR OPINION?

1. The Trapp family loved the outdoors. Do you spend much time outdoors? What are some of your favorite things you do outdoors?

2. Do you think it would be fun for all the members of a family to work together? What things do you think would be enjoyable? What problems might come up?

IEOH MING PEI

Will you make us leave?
Will we have to leave our homes again?
Mr. Pei answered their questions.
He made their lives better.
How did he do it?

a change for the better

A hot day People were everywhere. Some sat on their stoops. Others filled the sidewalk. It was a hot day. The temperature kept rising. It was already ninety-two degrees.

Youngsters in the street The youngsters did not seem to mind the heat. The small children ran about. They played a game. They ran around the parked cars. Older boys stood in the street. They tried to play a game of stickball. It was hopeless! Each time a car came, they had to stop.

The ghetto This part of the city was not very pleasant. It was a ghetto (*GET-oh*). There was very little to be proud of here. There were no parks, playgrounds, or swimming pools. Telephone poles lined the streets. There were no trees to give shade. The buildings were all old. The streets were noisy and dirty. Rats and roaches were everywhere. This was New York City's Bedford-Stuyvesant area.

The architect A well-dressed man walked down the street. He looked at everything. He took notes on all he saw. His name was Ieoh Ming Pei (*IY-ek MING PAY*). He was an architect (*ARK-uh-tekt*). He had a job to do.

This area was part of an urban-renewal (*UR-ben ree-NEW-ul*) program. I. M. Pei was the man in charge of this program. He had some new ideas. He wanted to change many things. He hoped to solve some of the problems of living in large cities.

The news of Mr. Pei's arrival spread fast. Soon, a crowd had gathered. They followed the Chinese-American man. They wanted to know what was going on.

The people had many questions to ask. They were afraid. "Mr. Pei," one man shouted. "Are you going to do what the others have done? Will we lose our homes? Will you make us leave? Will we be forced to move away?"

Mr. Pei listened. He knew the people were upset. He was not the first to come here with new ideas. Others had come in the past. But they had only brought trouble. The blacks and Puerto Ricans were sorry they came. To the poor, urban renewal meant losing their homes. It meant moving away. New homes were built. Other people moved into these new homes. They were not poor. They could afford the higher rents.

For the first tenants (*TEN-entz*), life did not change. They only moved a few blocks away. Other old buildings became their new homes. All that was different was the name of the street.

Mr. Pei calmed the people down. He told them that they did not have to worry. This time it would be different. They would not lose their homes. They would not have to leave.

This urban-renewal program was to be different. I. M. Pei had some new ideas. He hoped to solve some of the problems of living in large cities.

China

Crowded cities were not new to Mr. Pei. He was born in Canton, China. Later, his family moved to Shanghai (SHANG-hiy). Shanghai was the largest city in China. Over ten million people lived there. Here, I. M. Pei spent his childhood.

I. M. lived in a beautiful home in Shanghai. He went to a good school. There was always plenty to eat.

A promise

His father was a banker. He wanted his son to some-day take over the bank. I. M., however, had different ideas. He wanted to be an architect. He had seen how the rich people in Shanghai lived. He also saw how the poor people lived. There was a big difference between the two. I. M. hoped to change all that. He promised to make life better for the poor people.

The United States

When he was eighteen, I. M. Pei came to the United States. He worked and studied hard. In 1939, he graduated from college. He became an architect.

I. M. did not return to his homeland. World War II kept him in the United States. He became a citizen.

Fame spreads quickly

I. M. Pei's fame as an architect spread quickly. He designed beautiful churches, schools, and underground shopping centers. His John F. Kennedy Memorial Library won him much praise. Yet, I. M. was not happy. He had not

kept his promise. He had not helped the poor people.

Finally, I. M. Pei got his chance. He would rebuild Bedford-Stuyvesant. It would not be an easy job. It would take lots of hard work.

A chance

I. M. used his new ideas. He did not work by himself. He asked the people of Bedford-Stuyvesant to help him.

The people help

The people were happy. For the first time, they were asked how they felt. They were now a part of the change. They were helping to plan their own community.

Mr. Pei's plan was a simple one. The old buildings were not torn down. Instead, they were rebuilt. New lighting, walls, and ceilings were put in.

Mr. Pei's plan

The streets also changed. They became a place of beauty. Many of the streets were closed off. Parking lots were put in at each end. The rest of the street was turned into a garden. Statues (*STAH-chewz*), fountains (*FOWN-tenz*), and benches were put in. Soon pigeons (*PIH-ginz*), flowers, and grass appeared. They took the place of the black tar streets.

The streets

I. M. Pei did his job well. He proved cities could be places of beauty. He showed that change did not have to mean destruction (dee-*STRUK-shun*). His changes were for the better.

A change for the better

ACTIVITIES

2. The people in the ghetto were:

   a) rich.

   b) old.

   c) poor.

3. I. M. Pei hoped to solve the problems of living in:

   a) small towns.

   b) large cities.

   c) China.

4. In the past, urban renewal was:

   a) liked by the poor.

   b) disliked by the poor.

   c) done in small towns.

5. As a child, I. M. Pei was:

   a) poor.

   b) rich.

   c) hungry.

6. I. M. Pei's father was a (an):

   a) architect.

   b) banker.

   c) gardener.

7. I. M. Pei made a promise. It was to:

    a) come to America.

    b) be an architect.

    c) help the poor people.

8. In 1939, I. M. Pei:

    a) came to the United States.

    b) graduated from college.

    c) moved to Shanghai.

9. After college, I. M. Pei:

    a) went to China.

    b) stayed in the United States.

    c) moved to Shanghai.

10. I. M. Pei's plan was to:

    a) put up new buildings.

    b) rebuild the old buildings.

    c) tear everything down.

DO YOU KNOW THE MEANING?

1. "There were no trees to give shade." The opposite of shade is:

    a) hot.

    b) sunny.

    c) cool.

2. "Rats and roaches were everywhere." A roach is a (an):

    a) insect.

    b) spider.

    c) snake.

3. "This area was part of an urban-renewal program." Urban means having to do with:

    a) farms.

    b) countries.

    c) cities.

4. "They could afford the higher <u>rents</u>." Rent is money you pay for something that is:

    a) bought.

    b) used.

    c) old.

5. "He wanted to be an <u>architect</u>." An architect designs:

    a) buildings.

    b) cars.

    c) statues.

6. "I. M. did not return to his <u>homeland</u>." A homeland is a country where a person:

    a) spent his childhood.

    b) was raised.

    c) was born.

7. "I. M. Pei's <u>fame</u> as an architect spread quickly." Fame means to be:

    a) well-known.

    b) unknown.

    c) rich.

8. "Statues, <u>fountains</u>, and benches were put in." A fountain is usually filled with:

    a) grass.

    b) water.

    c) animals.

9. "Soon <u>pigeons</u>, flowers, and grass appeared." A pigeon is a:

    a) tree.

    b) plant.

    c) bird.

WHAT DO
YOU THINK?

1. Why did the youngsters not mind the heat?

2. Why were there so few trees in the ghetto?

3. Why did Mr. Pei take notes on things he saw?

4. Why did Bedford-Stuyvesant need urban renewal?

5. Why did people follow Mr. Pei?

6. Why were there so many people in Shanghai?

7. Why did Mr. Pei want his son to be a banker?

8. Why did I. M. Pei come to the United States?

9. Why did World War II keep I. M. Pei in the United States?

10. Why did I. M. Pei's plan work?

HAVE YOU
EVER
WONDERED?

1. How do you play stickball?

2. What does an architect do?

3. What are the problems of large cities?

4. What do large cities have to offer?

5. What is the most populated country in the world?

6. What is the Great Wall of China?

7. How is Chinese writing different from English?

8. What are some Chinese foods?

9. How do you use chop sticks?

WHAT IS
YOUR OPINION?

1. Do you think having a nice place to live plays an important part in making people happy? Explain your answer.

2. What are some ways in which the government can help poor people?

ARTHUR ASHE

The boys were waiting.
Arthur tried to run.
It was too late.
He could not get away.
What could Arthur do?

teacher's pet

The school empties The three o'clock bell rang. The doors of Richmond Junior High School opened. Hundreds of happy teenagers ran out of the building. They moved in all directions.

In a matter of seconds the school was empty. The noise and laughter were gone. All seemed peaceful and quiet.

A group waited A group of boys did not go home. They stood under a tree. The leader put his knife into the tree. "We'll get him today," he said. "He won't get a chance to run away. We'll show him what we think of a teacher's pet."

The smallest boy laughed. "Where is he?" he asked. "I'll bet he's with one of his teacher friends."

The boy they were after was Arthur Ashe. He was still in the building. But he was not talking to one of his teachers. He was in the principal's office.

The principal's office The principal spoke softly. "I have something to tell you," he said. "You're not going to like it."

Arthur sunk into the big leather chair. His mouth was dry. What did the principal mean? Had he done something wrong? Were his marks poor? What could it be?

The principal put his hand on Arthur's shoulder. He said, "I'm taking you off the baseball team."

The principal's decision

The boy was angry. "What do you mean?" he shouted. "I'm a good pitcher! The team needs me. Just this week I pitched a good job of relief! Don't punish me like this. Take me off the tennis team instead!"

The principal walked slowly to his desk. He gave the boy a chance to calm down. "You are not being punished," he said. "You are the best tennis player our school has ever had. This is why I must do this. I want you to spend all your time on tennis."

The principal's reason

The boy lowered his head sadly. "The principal doesn't understand," he thought. "Doesn't he know what tennis is doing to me? It's crazy! I don't know what to do. The teachers like my tennis playing. They always praise me. When they do, the boys call me names. They call me a teacher's pet and a sissy. I wish they would all leave me alone."

Problems with tennis

Arthur slowly closed the principal's door. He headed home. He knew his father was waiting.

Outside, the boys were waiting.

"Hey, sissy Ashe!" they shouted. "You want some help with your homework? Come here Ashey boy. We'll show you how to do homework."

Arthur is attacked

Arthur tried to run. It was too late. He could not get away. One of the boys grabbed his books. He threw them to his friend. "Hey, cut it out!" Arthur cried. "Let me have my books back."

"Here they are. Catch!" laughed one of the boys. The books flew through the air.

Arthur knelt (*NELT*) down to pick his books up. The boys jumped on him. They poured red ink on him and his books. They tried to rip his shirt off. Just then a teacher came out of the building. The older boy saw the teacher. He yelled to his friends. "Let's get out of here."

They ran away shouting. "Hey, sissy Ashe, you better get home quick. It's after three. Your daddy must be wondering why you're late."

At home with his father

At home, Arthur's father and younger brother were waiting. Mr. Ashe was sad to hear what happened. He wished the boy's mother was still alive. Her quiet manner always helped. She made big problems seem small.

Arthur's rise to fame

Time passed. Arthur's problems went away. The boys stopped calling him names. He became a hero. Everyone talked about his tennis playing. At the age of fourteen he already was one of the best players in our country. In 1961, he was the number two player on the U.C.L.A. team. In 1963, he was picked to be on the United States Davis Cup Team. He was the first black person ever chosen for the team. At twenty-two he was the second best player in the United States. He was also the sixth best in the world.

Arthur comes home

On February 4, 1966, the teacher's pet came home. Richmond, Virginia, celebrated "Arthur Ashe Day." Arthur rode in an open car. The streets were crowded. People shouted and cheered. Many in the crowd ran after him. They tried to touch him. They asked for his autograph (*AW-to-graf*).

Chased again

It seemed strange to Arthur. He thought of the time he was chased as a boy. Now he was being chased again. But this time it was for another reason.

ACTIVITIES

Arthur had trouble when he was a boy. Much of it came because:

DID YOU GET THE MAIN IDEA?

a) he liked playing baseball.

b) his mother died.

c) he did not like sports.

d) he was called a teacher's pet.

WHAT IS THE CORRECT ORDER?

1. Arthur leaves school.

2. The teacher comes out.

3. The 3 o'clock bell rings.

4. Arthur goes home.

5. The principal speaks to Arthur.

6. Red ink is poured on Arthur's books.

IS IT RIGHT OR WRONG?

1. Arthur was in elementary school.

2. Arthur was taken off the tennis team.

3. The teachers liked his tennis playing.

4. In 1961, he was picked to be on the United States Davis Cup Team.

5. "Arthur Ashe Day" was celebrated in Richmond, Virginia.

1. Arthur started playing tennis in:
   a) kindergarten.
   b) junior high school.
   c) high school.

2. The principal took Arthur off the:
   a) football team.
   b) baseball team.
   c) tennis team.

3. The boys were after Arthur because he was:
   a) a bully.
   b) fat.
   c) teacher's pet.

4. Arthur was attacked by the boys with:
   a) a knife.
   b) a gun.
   c) red ink.

5. The fight ended when one of the boys saw:
   a) a teacher.
   b) the principal.
   c) a policeman.

6. Arthur lived with his:
   a) mother and father.
   b) father and sister.
   c) brother and father.

7. Arthur's hometown is:
   a) Raleigh.
   b) New York.
   c) Richmond.

8. The United States Davis Cup team is a:
- **a)** tennis team.
- **b)** baseball team.
- **c)** football team.

9. When Arthur was chased in 1966 it was because:
- **a)** he was a hero.
- **b)** he was a sissy.
- **c)** he was the mayor.

10. Arthur's rise to fame started when he was:
- **a)** 22 years old.
- **b)** 18 years old.
- **c)** 14 years old.

DO YOU KNOW THE MEANING?

1. "The leader put a knife into the tree." The opposite of leader is someone who:
- **a)** follows.
- **b)** fights.
- **c)** belongs.

2. "Arthur sank into the big leather chair." Leather is made from:
- **a)** man-made fabrics.
- **b)** animal skins.
- **c)** trees.

3. "Just this week I pitched a good game of relief." To relieve someone is to:
- **a)** leave alone.
- **b)** give help.
- **c)** replace.

4. "Take me off the tennis team instead." Instead means:
- **a)** in place of.
- **b)** also.
- **c)** later.

5. "They praise me." Praise means to:

    a) dislike.

    b) approve.

    c) follow.

6. "Her quiet manner always helped." Manner means:

    a) sound.

    b) voice.

    c) way.

7. "He became a hero." A hero is someone who is:

    a) a teacher's pet.

    b) looked up to.

    c) hated.

WHAT DO YOU THINK?

1. Why didn't Arthur fight back?

2. Why did the other children call him a sissy?

3. How did the principal make his decision?

4. Why did Arthur want to play baseball?

5. Why did Richmond celebrate "Arthur Ashe Day"?

HAVE YOU EVER WONDERED?

1. What does *love* mean in tennis?

2. How does a person win a game of tennis?

3. How much does a professional tennis player make?

4. What does *Forest Hills* mean to a tennis player?

5. What does a *set* mean in tennis?

WHAT IS YOUR OPINION?

1. Would you like to become a famous person? Do you think life is easier or harder for a famous person like Arthur Ashe?

2. Everyone likes to be treated well by people his or her own age. Do you think it is fair to dislike a teacher's pet?

JULIE ANDREWS

The laughter stopped.
All at once there was a buzzing sound.
It came from the sky!
It was a bomb!
What could the people do?

the voice in the shelter

Everything stopped   There was a loud screeching (*SKREE-ching*) sound. It blasted through the air. It was the sound of a siren (*SIY-ren*).

Everything seemed to stop. The people of Beckenham, England listened. They looked at the sky. Somewhere up there was a twenty-five foot bomb. It was moving at three hundred sixty miles an hour. It was coming at them.

The buzzing sound   Everyone listened for a buzzing sound. That sound meant danger. It told of the nearness of the bomb. Soon it would crash. There would be a loud noise. Its ton of explosives (*ex-PLO-sivz*) would blow up.

People ran in all directions. They looked for a place to hide. They ran like ants. They looked for shelters (*SHEL-terz*). Here they could wait for the danger to pass.

A part of their lives   The people were used to this. Raids (*RAYDZ*) and shelters were a part of their lives. Their country was at war. The bomb was coming from Germany.

In the shelter   The shelter was filled. People made themselves comfortable (*KUM-fur-tuh-bul*). Some of them brought blankets. They made beds on the cold floor. Some women took out their sewing. Others prayed quietly.

"I wonder how long we will be?" asked one of the girls.

One of the mothers laughed. "I don't know," she said. "But I hope not long. It better be a short raid. My supper is on the stove."

The laughter stopped. All at once there was a buzzing sound. Everyone knew what it meant. A bomb was coming.

A bomb was coming

"Is it coming near us?" someone yelled. "Where is it?" Everyone looked at an eight year old girl. She had binoculars (*biy-NOK-you-lerz*). She was looking at the sky. "I think it will miss!" she said. "It's heading for the open field. It should land down the street."

The buzzing grew louder. The people sat quietly. They waited. There was nothing they could do. All was silent. A mother hugged her baby. She quietly rocked back and forth. An old lady held tightly to her cross. Her lips moved in silent prayer.

They could do nothing

Many of the people were afraid. They wondered, "Was today the day? Would the bomb hit their shelter? Would they all be killed?"

People were afraid

The buzzing reached its loudest point. The people held their breath. Then it happened! Silence! Nothing but silence!

The bomb landed

The bomb had landed. It did not go off. For the moment they were saved.

The girl with the binoculars

A man named Ted Andrews stood up. "That was a close one," he said. "I think we can rest a while." He looked at the girl with the binoculars. "Here Julie," he shouted. "Take this whistle (WIS-ul). Use it if any more of those bombs comes our way."

Come on, cheer up!

Ted picked up his guitar. He stood before the frightened crowd. "Let's forget about those *buzzers*," he said. "Come on, cheer up. Let's sing our troubles away." His wife Barbara helped. She moved about. She got the people to join in the song. It did not take long. Soon the shelter was filled with song.

Her thoughts were someplace else

Young Julie Andrews looked at the sky. She was not singing. Her thoughts were someplace else. She looked at Ted. "He thinks he's really something," she thought. "I'll bet he'll make me sing. I don't want to. I'm afraid of all those people. Oh how I wish my real father was here."

An unhappy girl

Julie was not a happy girl. When she was five her parents were divorced. Julie became a problem. Who would take her? Where would she live?

Julie was sent to live with her father. She did not stay there long. Her father could not care for her. She was too much work. Julie was sent back to her mother. There Julie met her stepfather.

Unwanted

Nothing seemed to go right. Everything and everyone seemed to be against her. She hated her house. She disliked the neighborhood. She was lonely. Her mother was always busy. She never had time for her. She did not like her stepfather very much. He made her feel unwanted.

No friends

Julie was not a pretty girl. She had no friends. Most girls her age met other children in school. They made friends easily. Julie never could. She was never in one place long enough. Barbara and Ted Andrews were singers. They had an act. They traveled a great deal. Julie had to go with them.

Julie forgot her troubles. She looked up at the sky. She had a job to do. "What's the use," she thought. "Worrying won't change anything."

Without knowing it, Julie began to hum. Words came to her lips. Soon she was singing out loud.

All eyes turned on the plain-looking girl. They listened. Her voice was beautiful. Julie's voice was different. It was clear. It reached notes no one else's voice could.

The beautiful voice

In time, Julie's voice made her famous. However, Julie had to work hard to become a success. She struggled for many years. Her work finally paid off. She became a star.

Julie came to the United States. She starred on the Broadway stage. She appeared on television. She was very popular. She starred in many motion pictures. *Mary Poppins* and *The Sound of Music* are two of her most famous movies.

In the United States

Julie's career continued to rise. Her name became known to millions. Her voice could now be heard around the world.

Known to millions

ACTIVITIES

DID YOU GET THE MAIN IDEA?

Many things made Julie unhappy. Which of these did not?

a) her parents divorce.

b) her singing.

c) feeling unwanted.

d) having no friends.

WHAT IS THE CORRECT ORDER?

1. The bomb lands.

2. Julie comes to the United States.

3. Julie's parents are divorced.

4. Julie stars in *The Sound of Music*.

5. Julie goes to live with her father.

6. Julie sings in the shelter.

IS IT RIGHT OR WRONG?

1. The bomb came from England.

2. Julie's family traveled a great deal.

3. Julie always had friends.

4. Julie was not a pretty girl.

5. Julie's parents were divorced when she was eight.

DO YOU REMEMBER?

1. What kind of sound did the siren make?

a) low.

b) screeching.

c) pleasant.

2. The buzzing sound meant the bomb was:

    a) near.

    b) far.

    c) gone.

3. People went into the shelters to:

    a) pray.

    b) sleep.

    c) hide.

4. The bomb:

    a) went off.

    b) did not go off.

    c) stayed in the air.

5. Ted was Julie's:

    a) real father.

    b) stepfather.

    c) brother.

6. Ted played the:

    a) piano.

    b) violin.

    c) guitar.

7. How old was Julie when her parents were divorced?

    a) eight.

    b) three.

    c) five.

8. Who made Julie feel unwanted?

    a) her brother.

    b) an old lady.

    c) her stepfather.

9. Julie's voice was different. It was:

   a) clear.

   b) loud.

   c) dull.

10. Julie came from:

   a) the United States.

   b) England.

   c) Germany.

1. "That sound meant <u>danger</u>." The opposite of danger is:

   a) safety.

   b) fear.

   c) pain.

2. "She had <u>binoculars</u>." People use binoculars to:

   a) make things look smaller.

   b) make things look bigger.

   c) make things look clearer.

3. "A mother <u>hugged</u> her baby." To hug means to:

   a) hold.

   b) feed.

   c) dress.

4. "Julie began to <u>hum</u>." To hum means to:

   a) whistle.

   b) sing without moving your lips.

   c) sing out loud.

5. "She <u>struggled</u> for many years." To struggle means to:

   a) give up.

   b) take it easy.

   c) try hard.

6. She starred in many <u>motion pictures</u>." A motion picture is a:

    a) Broadway play.

    b) movie.

    c) television show.

1. Why did the people run into the shelters?

2. Why did some people bring blankets to the shelter?

3. Why did Julie use binoculars to find the bomb?

4. Why didn't the bomb go off?

5. Why did Ted want the people to sing?

6. Why did Julie want to be with her real father?

7. Why did her mother have little time for her?

WHAT DO
YOU THINK?

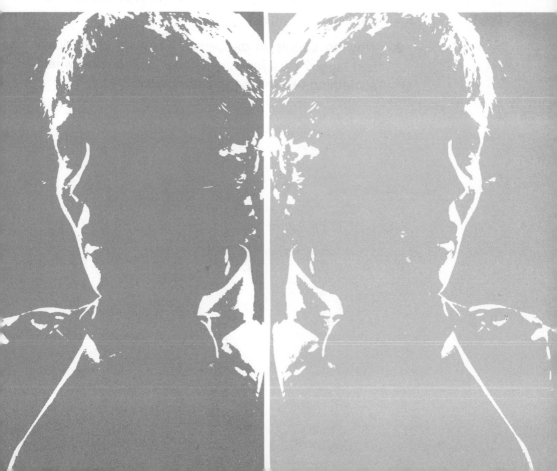

HAVE YOU EVER WONDERED?

1. How does a bomb cause damage?

2. How did the war between England and Germany begin?

3. What was it like to be in London during World War II?

4. What kind of bomb could travel so far?

5. How did the bomb get into the air?

6. How are we protected from bombs and missels?

7. In the picture *Mary Poppins*, Julie flew through the air. How do film makers do this?

8. How are cartoons made?

WHAT IS YOUR OPINION?

1. Would you like it if your family traveled a lot? What are some advantages of traveling? Can you think of any disadvantages?

2. Why do people in dangerous situations try to joke and laugh? Can you think of a serious moment when something like this happened to you?

JOAN BAEZ

The old lady's hands dug into the garbage.
She searched for scraps of food.
She found the package.
She opened it and left it.
Why didn't she eat the cake Joan left?

a country's conscience

Wondering   The young girl looked out the window. She watched the garbage can below. "Would the old lady return?" she wondered. "Would she eat the cake in the package? Would she be happy?"

Joan Baez (*BY-ez*) did not have long to wait. A trembling figure came into view. Dirty rags covered her stooped body. The old woman had returned.

The old lady   The old lady was a sad sight. Her face was worn and thin. Her wrinkled (*RINK-uld*) skin seemed to hang on her old bones. Every step she took seemed to cause her pain. Her hands shook. They grabbed the wall. She stopped to rest for a minute.

The old lady's eyes searched the street. They looked up to Joan's window. Then, they fell to the garbage can.

The package   The old lady's hands dug into the garbage. She searched for scraps of food. The package caught her attention. She opened it. Then she put it down. She did not eat it. Instead, she dug deeper into the can.

She ate quickly   The old lady was in luck today. She found some potato peels and chicken bones. The food went into her mouth. She ate quickly. After a few seconds, she was gone. The package remained. The cake was not eaten.

Joan did not understand. "Why didn't she eat the cake?" she wondered. "Didn't she trust me? Was she afraid?"

There was much Joan did not understand. Her trip to Baghdad (*BAG-dad*), Iraq was to have been fun. Instead, it was sad. All around her was sorrow. People were starving. Children were dying. They lay in the street screaming for food. Yet, no one helped. People just walked by. They did not seem to care. *Baghdad*

To Joan, sorrow and hardship seemed to be everywhere. Although only eleven years old, Joan had been to many places. Her father's job forced the family to move a lot. They had lived in New York, California, Iraq, Boston, and Paris. *Sorrow and hardship*

Joan's own childhood was full of sorrow. She was very lonely. She learned how cruel others can be. The children in school called her names. They made fun of her Mexican background. They made jokes about her dark skin. They refused to play with her. *Joan's childhood*

Joan hoped for a better world. But being young there was very little she could do. Her sorrow and that of others were out of her control. She wished she could change things. But she did not know how. *Out of her control*

When Joan was twelve she learned to play the guitar. This changed her whole life. People liked to listen to her. They liked her songs and her voice. *The guitar*

After high school, Joan's singing became her whole life. She sang in coffee houses. She appeared at gatherings and festivals (*FES-tuh-vulz*). She worked *A new life*

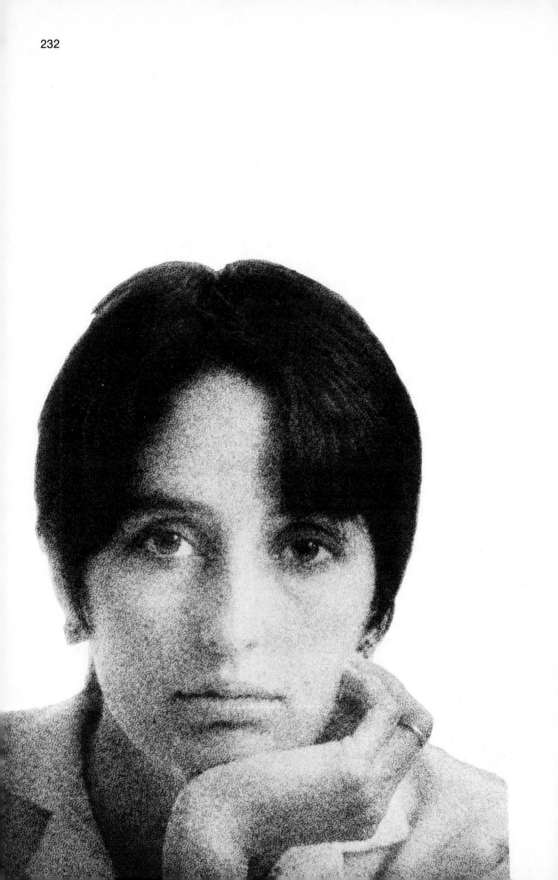

hard. Her fame spread. Soon she became a success. She was the country's leading folksinger. For many people Joan was also something else. She was the "country's conscience (*KON-shens*)."

As a girl, there was little Joan could do about the things that bothered her. Now everything had changed. People listened to her. They wanted to hear what she had to say. Now she could talk about the things that bothered her. Now she had a chance to change things.

Everything changed

Joan spoke on many issues (*ISH-youz*). She raised many questions. "Today," she said, "there is a real need for peace. The people of the world look for understanding. Yet, our planet's history is one of hate. It is a long record of wars and fights. Why? Is it because we have not tried enough? What has happened to human life? Are flags and countries more important than people? Have people become lazy? Are they afraid to speak out? Must injustice (*in-JUS-tis*) and cruelty remain forever?"

Joan spoke out

Joan did more than just talk. She acted. She marched in demonstrations (*dem-un-STRAY-shunz*). She raised money for what she believed in. She even went to jail.

Joan's actions

In 1967, Joan took part in an anti-war demonstration. It was at a California draft board. She and others were trying to stop men from going to fight in Vietnam. Joan was arrested. She spent her Christmas in jail.

Christmas

In 1972, Joan led another protest. It was called "A Ring Around the Congress." Like all her actions, this was a peaceful one. Women and children simply joined hands. They made a ring around the Capitol building. They spoke to their congressmen. "Look," they said, "we are women and children. We can't stand it any more. Stop this fighting. End this war. Stop this hatred."

A Ring Around the Congress

Joan Baez tried to do more than end a war. She wanted to change other things as well. She wanted to bring peace to a troubled world. "Every country needs a conscience," she said. "People have to speak out against what is wrong. If everyone does, life will change. It will have meaning. Things will change for the better."

Joan's dream

ACTIVITIES

DID YOU GET THE MAIN IDEA? Joan believes a country needs a conscience to:

    a) hold demonstrations.

    b) fight against wars.

    c) change things for the better.

    d) fight crime.

WHAT IS THE CORRECT ORDER?

1. Joan spends Christmas in prison.

2. Joan goes to Baghdad.

3. Joan learns to play the guitar.

4. Joan leads a "Ring Around the Congress."

5. Joan becomes a success.

6. The old lady leaves the cake.

IS IT RIGHT OR WRONG?

1. The old lady was rich.

2. Joan saw much happiness in Baghdad.

3. Joan was against the war in Vietnam.

4. Joan's family moved a lot.

5. Joan had light-colored skin.

DO YOU REMEMBER?

1. Joan watched the old lady from:

    a) a window.

    b) the street.

    c) a doorway.

2. The old lady ate:

   a) cake.

   b) bread.

   c) scraps.

3. Joan found people starving in:

   a) New York.

   b) Boston.

   c) Baghdad.

4. Joan traveled a lot because:

   a) she liked it.

   b) of her father's job.

   c) she was searching.

5. Joan's childhood was:

   a) happy.

   b) sad.

   c) dull.

6. Young Joan could not change things because:

   a) she did not know how.

   b) she had no money.

   c) no one would listen.

7. When Joan was twelve, she learned to play the:

   a) guitar.

   b) violin.

   c) piano.

8. Joan became the country's leading:

   a) demonstrator.

   b) speaker.

   c) folksinger.

9. Joan was arrested because she:
   a) stole something.

   b) took part in a demonstration.

   c) killed someone.

10. "A Ring Around the Congress" was made up of:

    a) men and women.

    b) women and children.

    c) men and children.

DO YOU KNOW THE MEANING?

1. "Dirty rags covered her <u>stooped</u> body." To stoop means to:
   a) stand straight.

   b) bend over.

   c) lay flat.

2. "Her <u>wrinkled</u> skin seemed to hang on her old bones." The opposite of wrinkled is:
   a) smooth.

   b) bumpy.

   c) lumpy.

3. "People were <u>starving</u>." To starve means to be:
   a) very thirsty.

   b) very hungry.

   c) very poor.

4. "To Joan, sorrow and <u>hardship</u> seemed to be everywhere." Hardship is something that is difficult to:
   a) keep.

   b) bear.

   c) hear.

5. "She learned how <u>cruel</u> others can be." The opposite of cruel is:
   a) friendly.

   b) lonely.

   c) strange.

6. "Her sorrow and that of others were out of her control." To control something means to:

   a) have charge of.

   b) ask about.

   c) ruin it.

7. "Joan spoke on many issues." An issue is:

   a) a stage.

   b) an argument.

   c) a topic.

8. "She marched in demonstrations." To demonstrate means to:

   a) hide.

   b) fight.

   c) show.

9. "In 1967, Joan took part in another protest." To protest means to:

   a) object.

   b) agree.

   c) ask.

10. "Every country needs a conscience." A conscience tells a person:

   a) right from wrong.

   b) his past.

   c) his future.

WHAT DO
YOU THINK?

1. Why did Joan leave cake for the old lady?

2. Why did the old lady look sad?

3. Why didn't the old lady eat the cake?

4. Why didn't anyone help the starving children of Baghdad?

5. Why did children in school pick on Joan?

6. Why did Joan wish she could change things?

7. How did the guitar change Joan's whole life?

8. How did Joan's fame spread so quickly?

9. Why did everyone listen to Joan when she was a success?

HAVE YOU
EVER
WONDERED?

1. What is life like in other parts of the world?

2. Why do people live longer in the United States?

3. What happens to a person's body when he is starving?

4. What causes people to hate others?

5. How is a folksinger different from a popular singer?

6. How is a demonstration organized?

7. What is an electric guitar?

8. Why does a folksinger usually travel a great deal?

WHAT IS
YOUR OPINION?

1. Do you think a person should speak out even if people disagree with him? Why or why not?

2. What are some of our country's problems? What are some things that could be done to solve these problems?

EERO SAARINEN

The telegram is here!
It's the news you've been waiting for!
The telegram was opened.
The name was read.
Who had the judges picked?
Was it the father or the son?

like father, like son

The door bell   The door bell rang. A young man stood outside. He had an envelope in his hand.

Mrs. Saarinen (*SAR-uh-nin*) hurried from the kitchen. She opened the door. "Yes," she said. "May I help you?"

The telegram   "I have a telegram for Mr. Saarinen. Sign here, please," the young man said.

Mrs. Saarinen signed the paper. She looked at the envelope. It was from St. Louis. She hurried inside. "Eero (*EER-oh*)! Eliel (*EL-ee-el*)!" she called. "Come quickly! It's here. It's the news you've been waiting for."

Mrs. Saarinen went into the living room. Eero and Eliel came to meet her. Eliel was her husband. Eero was her son.

Who would it be?   The two men stared at each other. They were uneasy. One of their names was in the telegram. Each man wondered "Is it me?"

Rivals   Father and son were rivals (*RIY-vulz*). Both were architects. They were both trying for the same project. It was to design a monument (*MON-you-ment*). The monument would overlook the bank of the Mississippi River near St. Louis.

Both men sent in designs. The judges had made their choice. The long wait was over. Which architect would it be? Would it be the father or the son?

The wait was over

"You open it," said Eliel to his wife. "Tell us who it is!"

Mrs. Saarinen opened the envelope. She looked at the words. The two men waited. She read, "The man chosen is Eliel Saarinen."

The name was read

The family celebrated (*SEL-uh-bray-ted*) the good news. Eero tried to act happy. It was not easy. He toasted (*TOHS-ted*) his father. He wished him luck. They all drank champagne (*sham-PAYN*).

The family celebrates

Eero tried not to show his feelings. He was disappointed. He wished his name was in the telegram.

Disappointed

Having a famous father was not easy. Eliel was known all over the world. Architects admired him. He was respected.

A famous father

Eero was expected to be like his father. His work was questioned. It was always compared to his father's. It was never accepted on its own. Sometimes the young

Eero's work

man felt like shouting. "Why won't they accept *me*?" he thought. "It was this way in Finland. It is the same in the United States. Why must I always be known as the son of Eliel Saarinen?"

Not an equal

Eero was a partner in his father's firm. It was only a title. He was not an equal. Saarinen architecture meant Eliel's work. The father was the one people talked about. Eero was just his son. He was expected to have the same ideas.

Eero's problem

Eero had a problem. He wanted to be on his own. He wanted to break away from his father. Yet, he knew he could not. He owed a lot to his father. His father had always stood by him. Eero learned all he knew from his father.

Finland

Eero grew up in Finland. He was happy there. The family spent much time in their large studio-living room. Eero liked looking out the large window. Below was a beautiful Finnish lake.

The boy had talent

Young Eero liked to draw. Mr. Saarinen helped him. He was never too busy for his son. He took special interest in everything Eero did. Soon his son was sketching (*SKEH-ching*). Later Eero worked with clay and stone. He had talent!

An important lesson

In Finland, Eero learned an important lesson. His father taught it to him. Eero tried to do well in everything. His father stopped him. He said, "Son, no one can do well in everything. One can only do what one is able to do. No one can ask for more. There is only one exception. That is if you have talent. A person with talent must work extra hard. He must make his dream come true."

The family did not stay in Finland. There was a lack *A new job* of work. Mr. Saarinen sent drawings to many places. He hoped to get a job. One place offered him $20,000. It was in the United States. Mr. Saarinen took the job. He brought his family to New York.

Eero did not like New York. The thirteen year old *New York* hated the noise and the traffic. He wondered how anyone could sleep. Manhattan never got quiet.

Eero was glad to leave New York. The Midwest *A new home* was much quieter. They moved to a place near Detroit (*dee-TROYT*). Here his father set up a school. Later, he started his architecture (*ARK-uh-tek-chur*) firm.

When Eero was nineteen, he left his new home. He *Paris* wanted to be a sculptor (*SKULP-ter*). He studied in Paris. After a year he changed his mind. Eero returned to the United States.

Eero joined his father. He worked on many projects. He waited for his chance. He wanted to do something on his own.

The young man was in for a surprise. It came a *A surprise* few days after the telegram had arrived. A new telegram came. There had been a mistake. The wrong name had been printed on the first telegram. The man they wanted for the job was Eero Saarinen.

Eero's life took on new meaning. Now he showed *New meaning* what he could do. His 640-foot arch in St. Louis made him famous. It became the new gateway to the west. He designed the first jet airport. He invented *mobile lounges*.

The young man became one of the world's leading *Saarinen architecture* architects. Saarinen architecture was well-known. But now it was different. It was the son, and not the father, they were talking about. Eero Saarinen had made it.

ACTIVITIES

DID YOU GET THE MAIN IDEA?

The second telegram made Eero happy because:

a) it gave a job to his father.

b) he could now go to Paris.

c) he could now do something on his own.

d) he was made a partner.

WHAT IS THE CORRECT ORDER?

1. The second telegram arrives.

2. Eero's father teaches him an important lesson.

3. Eero goes to Paris.

4. The Saarinens move to the Midwest.

5. The 640-foot arch goes up in St. Louis.

6. Eero moves to New York.

IS IT RIGHT OR WRONG?

1. Eero was Mrs. Saarinen's son.

2. The first telegram made Eero happy.

3. Eero and Eliel were partners.

4. Eero stayed in Paris for six years.

5. Eero invented *mobile lounges*.

DO YOU REMEMBER?

1. The first telegram was for:

a) Eero.

b) Mrs. Saarinen.

c) Eliel.

2. The telegrams came from:

   a) St. Louis.

   b) Paris.

   c) New York.

3. Eero and Eliel were:

   a) sculptors.

   b) architects.

   c) brothers.

4. As a boy, Eero looked out a large window at:

   a) a lake.

   b) tall buildings.

   c) monuments.

5. Who taught Eero an important lesson?

   a) his mother.

   b) his father.

   c) a teacher.

6. Eliel brought his family to the United States because:

   a) he wanted to be a sculptor.

   b) he was offered a job.

   c) he wanted to travel.

7. Eero did not like New York because:

   a) it was noisy.

   b) he was homesick.

   c) of the tall buildings.

8. How old was Eero when he went to Paris?

   a) 13.

   b) 6.

   c) 19.

9. At first, Eero wanted to be:

   a) a sculptor.

   b) an architect.

   c) a painter.

10. Eero's 640-foot arch was built in:

    a) New York.

    b) St. Louis.

    c) Paris.

DO YOU KNOW THE MEANING?

1. "Father and son were <u>rivals</u>." Rivals are people who:

   a) want to change things.

   b) want the same thing.

   c) build monuments.

2. "It was to design a <u>monument</u>." A monument is a building:

   a) in the center of a town.

   b) that is very tall.

   c) built in memory of something.

3. "Both men sent in <u>designs</u>." A design is:

   a) a plan.

   b) a building.

   c) a letter.

4. "The family celebrated the good news." A celebration is a:

   a) prayer of thanks.

   b) fancy meal.

   c) special kind of party.

5. "He toasted his father." A toast is:

   a) saying things you don't mean.

   b) words said before drinking.

   c) a poem.

6. "They all drank champagne." Champagne is a type of:

   a) wine.

   b) juice.

   c) soda.

7. "It was always compared to his father's." To compare means to:

   a) make fun of.

   b) see how something is different.

   c) praise.

8. "Eero was a partner in his father's firm." A partner is a person who:

   a) works with someone.

   b) is a clerk.

   c) works for a relative.

9. "The family spent much time in their large studio–living room." A studio is a place where:

   a) people sleep.

   b) artists work.

   c) children play.

10. "There is only one <u>exception</u>." An exception is:

   a) something that is different.

   b) a person who is talented.

   c) a rule.

WHAT DO YOU THINK?

1. Why did the first telegram make the men uneasy?

2. Why did Eero try to act happy when he heard the news?

3. Why was Eliel admired and respected?

4. Why wasn't Eero really a partner?

5. Why was Eero expected to be like his father?

6. Why did Eero think he owed a lot to his father?

7. Why couldn't Eero get used to Manhattan?

8. Why did Eero's life take on new meaning after the second telegram?

HAVE YOU EVER WONDERED?

1. Where is Finland?

2. How do you send a telegram?

3. What does an architect do?

4. What is a *mobile lounge?*

5. How big must a jet airport be?

6. How do you travel through the St. Louis arch?

WHAT IS YOUR OPINION?

1. What benefits can a famous parent give to his child? What problems may result from having a famous parent?

2. How do you think Eliel felt when the second telegram arrived?

MELISSA HAYDEN

Then it happened!
Melissa fell to the ground.
The graceful ballerina was hurt.
The large gold curtain came down.
Was Melissa's career over?

the curtain came down

The crowd waits   The lights in the large hall grew dim. The London crowd grew quiet. Everyone waited. The ballet (*bah-LAY*) was about to begin.

The conductor (*kun-DUCK-tur*) entered. There was a small round of applause. He walked to his place before the orchestra (*OR-kiss-tra*). He raised his arms. He pointed to his violin section. The quiet was gone. Music filled the air. The big gold curtain rose silently.

The star ballerina   All eyes were on the stage. They watched the star ballerina. She was Melissa Hayden (*muh-LIS-ih HY-din*). A white spotlight shone on her. She wore a purple and green costume.

A pleased crowd   Everything was perfect. She danced as she had never danced before. Melissa was great. She seemed to float through the air. She and the music became one. The crowd was pleased. They applauded every move. She turned and jumped in perfect form. Everyone could see why this ballet was made just for her.

Melissa was happy. Her many years of hard work had paid off. Now she would get the credit she deserved.

Then it happened! Melissa fell to the ground. The graceful ballerina was hurt. The crowd watched in silence. The large gold curtain came down.

The curtain came down

Melissa lay on the floor. She could not move. She was knocked out. Someone shouted. "Make room! Give her air!"

Melissa could not move

One of the dancers leaned over. She began to breathe into Melissa's mouth. After a while the star awoke. Her eyes slowly opened.

Her eyes opened

Near Melissa was the cause of the fall. It came from some worker's clumsiness (*KLUM-zee-ness*). The floor had not been mopped. There was a puddle near her ballet slipper.

A worker's mistake

Was the show over? Was her career ended?

Melissa Hayden did not think so. The Canadian-born American was a fighter. She would not let a fall stop her. She had worked too hard. She was not going to give up now. "Bring up the curtain! I'm going on," she said.

I'm going on!

Melissa got to her feet. She continued to dance. She acted as if nothing had happened.

Loud applause

The ballet continued. Melissa finished the dance. The curtain came down again. There was loud appluase. It was for Melissa.

Her career rose after that performance. The London newspapers wrote about her. "She is great," they said. "She is one of the most promising stars in the ballet."

Melissa returned to the United States. She was a member of the New York City Ballet. Here she continued to dance. She thrilled audiences in many roles.

The New York City Ballet

Melissa's success did not come easily. Many years of practice were needed. Daily exercise was a part of her life. It was hard work.

Daily exercise

Melissa had to work harder than most dancers. She started her lessons late. She began in Canada when she was sixteen. It was difficult to catch up.

A late start

The young girl worked hard. She practiced every chance she had. Melissa went to class early. She stood

Before the wall mirror

before the wall mirror. She went through her routines (*REW-teenz*). Over and over she did them. After two hours she stopped. She waited for the other girls to come. Then her regular lesson began.

At home   She worked even harder at home. She rose at five each day. There was much to do. There were exercises. She had to get them right. Over and over she practiced.

Her practice paid off. Her muscles grew strong. She became more graceful. Her body moved freely.

Time to leave   By the time she was twenty, Melissa had learned all she could. She needed new teachers. She had to go to new schools. She would have to leave Canada.

She talked it over with her parents. She told them why she had to leave. They agreed.

Melissa took what little money she had. She came to the United States.

Something new each day   Melissa loved New York City. The ballet schools were excellent. Each day brought something new. She was happy. In just a few weeks, she had learned much.

Taking notes   Melissa forgot nothing. She kept notes. Each day she wrote down what she learned. Every evening she practiced the new steps.

Melissa was becoming a good dancer. It was what she always wanted to be.

Trouble   Then trouble came! Her money ran out. This meant no more lessons. It meant going home.

A job   Melissa did not give up. She found a way to stay. She got a job. It was at the Radio City Music Hall. She danced with the stage show. Here she made the money she needed.

Her new job was not easy. The hours were long. She did four shows a day. In between shows she took lessons. At the end of the day she was very tired.

Her reward   Melissa was rewarded. Her hard work paid off. She became "The Prima (*PREE-muh*) Ballerina of New York."

ACTIVITIES

Melissa was a fighter. She showed this by:

DID YOU GET THE MAIN IDEA?

- **a)** getting up after her fall.
- **b)** dancing gracefully.
- **c)** keeping notes.
- **d)** becoming the Prima Ballerina.

WHAT IS THE CORRECT ORDER?

1. Melissa comes to New York City.
2. Melissa falls to the floor.
3. Melissa gets a job at Radio City Music Hall.
4. Melissa gets up at five each morning.
5. Melissa starts taking ballet lessons.
6. Melissa leaves London.

IS IT RIGHT OR WRONG?

1. Melissa fell while dancing in New York.
2. Melissa had to work harder than most dancers.
3. The schools in Canada taught her all she knew.
4. Her parents would not let her leave Canada.
5. Melissa worked at the Radio City Music Hall.

DO YOU REMEMBER?

1. The conductor pointed to the:
   - **a)** brass section.
   - **b)** violin section.
   - **c)** drum section.

2. The big curtain was:
   a) gold.

   b) white.

   c) purple and green.

3. Melissa fell because she:
   a) was tired.

   b) slipped.

   c) tripped.

4. Melissa practiced early at school. She stopped after:
   a) one hour.

   b) two hours.

   c) five hours.

5. Melissa left Canada when she was:
   a) five.

   b) sixteen.

   c) twenty.

6. Melissa came to New York:
   a) because there were tall buildings.

   b) to work at the Music Hall.

   c) to learn more.

7. Melissa practiced nightly. She remembered every-thing because she:
   a) had a good memory.

   b) called the teacher.

   c) took notes.

8. Melissa almost had to leave the United States because:
   a) she fell on the stage.

   b) her money ran out.

   c) she learned all she could.

9. Melissa started taking ballet lessons when she was:
   a) a child.

   b) a teen-ager.

   c) an adult.

10. Melissa became the Prima Ballerina of:
  a) Canada.
  b) London.
  c) New York.

1. "The <u>conductor</u> entered." The conductor:
  a) is a ballet dancer.
  b) plays the violin.
  c) leads an orchestra.

2. "She wore a purple and green <u>costume</u>." A costume is:
  a) a pin.
  b) a ballet slipper.
  c) an outfit.

3. "The <u>graceful</u> ballerina was hurt." The opposite of graceful is:
  a) clumsy.
  b) silly.
  c) nervous.

4. "She <u>continued</u> to dance." To continue means to:
  a) begin.
  b) keep going.
  c) finish.

5. "She <u>thrilled</u> audiences in many roles." Thrilled means to be:
  a) excited.
  b) afraid.
  c) worried.

6. "<u>Daily</u> exercise was a part of her life." Daily means:
  a) always.
  b) every day.
  c) often.

7. "Melissa was <u>rewarded</u>." The opposite of rewarded is:

   a) punished.

   b) praised.

   c) paid.

WHAT DO YOU THINK?

1. Why did the lights in the large hall grow dim?

2. Why did Melissa seem to float through the air?

3. Why did the crowd watch in silence as she fell?

4. Why did one of the dancers breathe into Melissa's mouth?

5. Why did Melissa continue to dance after her fall?

6. Why did she have to practice so hard?

7. Why must a ballet dancer be graceful?

8. Why were the schools in New York better?

HAVE YOU EVER WONDERED?

1. Do you need a passport to go from Canada to the United States?

2. What is a *tutu?*

3. What are the five basic positions in ballet?

4. What is a *choreographer?*

5. Why is the *Nutcracker Suite* popular with children?

6. How does a person train to be a ballet dancer?

7. What things must a ballet dancer know?

WHAT IS YOUR OPINION?

1. Has anyone ever suffered because you were clumsy or sloppy? Have you ever suffered because of another person's clumsiness? Describe what happened. Did you learn a lesson from this? What was the lesson?

2. Do you think all people must work hard in order to succeed? Explain your answer.

ERIK ERIKSON

"Get out of here you long-haired freak!"
"Go back where you came from!"
Erik kept walking.
He did not try to talk with the men.
Why was he misunderstood?
Why was he hated?

who am i?

Dead trees   The sun moved overhead. Ripples (*RIP-ulz*) of hot air rose from the road. There was a sound of metal against wood. It was a chopping sound. Some men were clearing the road of dead trees.

The men worked hard. With each swing of the ax, their tempers grew shorter. Sweat poured from their bodies. Their muscles hurt.

The men stop   One of the men stopped digging. He poked the man next to him. "Look," he said. "Here comes that bum again." The other men stopped working. They looked down the road.

The youth   A long-haired blond youth appeared. He wore sandals and dungarees. He carried a pack over his shoulder. As he grew nearer, the men began to shout. "Get out of here you long-haired freak! Get a job! Make something of yourself! Go back where you came from!"

He did not stop   Erik Erikson kept walking. He did not stop. He did not try to talk with the men. He knew it was useless. They would not understand.

Not the first time   This was not the first time this had happened. It happened to Erik in the Black Forest of Germany. It was the same in the Alps. And now it was happening in Italy. It was always the same shouts. The language was different. But the hatred was the same.

People would not accept him. His hair and clothes angered them. They thought he should work instead of wander.

Not accepted

Erik was confused. Many things bothered him. The adult world frightened him. Being an adult meant accepting the world. It meant doing what everyone else did. It meant dressing a special way. Adults had to work. They stayed in one place.

Being an adult

Erik was not ready for this. He could not accept life as others knew it. He had many questions. "Who Am I? What is my purpose? What is life all about?"

Unanswered questions

Erik's biggest problem was himself. His early life was mixed up. His mother and stepfather had lied to him. They told him he was a German-Jew. He was told his name was Erik Homburger. But Erik's real father was Danish. His name was Erikson.

His biggest problem

Erik never saw his real father. He left before Erik was born. Erik's mother left Denmark and moved to Germany. Three years later she remarried.

His real father

These things were never told to Erik. Later, he found out. They disturbed him.

Erik's childhood was painful. He was not accepted. He had few friends. The Jewish boys called him names. They laughed at him. "You're no Jew!" they said. "Who ever heard of a blond-haired Jew? What Jew has blue eyes? You must be a Christian. Get out of here!"

Painful childhood

The German boys would not accept him either. Many of them hated Jews. They wanted no part of him.

Erik leaves home After high school, Erik left home. He wandered throughout Europe. As he traveled he painted and wrote. He tried to find himself in art. He searched for the answers to his problems.

Erik returns After five years, Erik returned home. His search was over. Many of his questions were answered. Now, he knew what he must do. He would become a psychiatrist (*suh-KIY-uh-trist*). In that way he could help others to find themselves. He would find the reasons for people's behavior.

In the United States Later, Erik came to the United States. Here he continued to work. He lived with the Sioux (SOO) and Yurok Indians. He studied their problems. He tried to help them.

His work Much of Erik's time was spent with the poor. He worked with farmers and ghetto children. Their childhood was of special interest to him. He found out all he could about them.

Early life important Erik learned much from his studies. He learned that a person's early life was very important. It played an important part in growing up.

The problems of life Erik found that each person has eight different problem times. The first comes when one is just a baby. The last comes when one is old. The problem in life is solving each. To do so, one has to believe in oneself. One has to be able to connect the past with the future. Many people did this. They were happy. They matured (*muh-TURD*).

The people Erik helped Some people could not solve their problems. They became confused. Some became mentally (*MEN-tuh-ly*) ill. These were the people Erik helped. He tried to help them face their problems. They needed to find themselves.

A famous book Erik wrote about what he learned. His work was printed in books and magazines. He wrote a famous book called *Childhood and Society*. It made him the leader in his field. It helped millions of people answer the question, "Who am I?"

ACTIVITIES

Erik found that the secret of a happy life was:

    a)   money.

    b)   solving ones problems.

    c)   traveling.

    d)   living with Indians.

DID YOU GET THE MAIN IDEA?

1. Erik comes to the United States.

2. Erik's mother remarries.

3. Erik travels in Italy.

4. Erik is called names in school.

5. Erik lives with the Sioux.

6. Erik graduates from high school.

WHAT IS THE CORRECT ORDER?

1. Erik spent his childhood in Denmark.

2. Erik went to high school in Germany.

3. Erik had brown eyes.

4. Erik worked with and studied rich people.

5. Erik counted eight problem times in life.

IS IT RIGHT OR WRONG?

1. The men who yelled at Erik were:

    a)   putting in a new sewer.

    b)   chopping down trees.

    c)   paving the road.

DO YOU REMEMBER?

2. Erik did not answer the men because:

    a) he knew it was useless.

    b) he was afraid.

    c) he did not hear them.

3. Erik was trying to find:

    a) himself.

    b) his mother.

    c) his father.

4. Erik's real father came from:

    a) Germany.

    b) Italy.

    c) Denmark.

5. Erik's mother remarried when Erik was:

    a) four years old.

    b) one year old.

    c) three years old.

6. The Jewish boys made fun of Erik because of:

    a) his religion.

    b) his looks.

    c) his name.

7. Erik traveled through Europe for:

    a) three years.

    b) four years.

    c) five years.

8. Erik became a:

    a) wood cutter.

    b) teacher.

    c) psychiatrist.

9. A psychiatrist is a person who works with:

   a) animals.

   b) happy people.

   c) unhappy people.

10. People found out about Erik's work because of his:

   a) travels.

   b) writings.

   c) talks.

1. "Ripples of hot air rose from the road." A ripple is what kind of wave?   **DO YOU KNOW THE MEANING?**

   a) big.

   b) small.

   c) giant.

2. "He wore sandals and dungarees." Sandals are worn on ones:

   a) hands.

   b) feet.

   c) head.

3. "They thought he should work instead of wander." To wander means to:

   a) stay in one place.

   b) move about.

   c) settle.

4. "The adult world frightened him." To be frightened means to be:

   a) angry.

   b) scared.

   c) lonely.

5. "Erik was <u>confused</u>." To be confused is to be:

    a)   mixed up.

    b)   lonely.

    c)   an Indian.

6. "He worked with farmers and <u>ghetto</u> children." People who live in a ghetto are:

   a) poor.

   b) rich.

   c) Indian.

7. "He was not <u>accepted</u>." To be accepted is to be:

   a) pushed over.

   b) left out.

   c) taken in.

8. "He <u>searched</u> for the answers to his problems." The opposite of search is:

   a) to find.

   b) to look for.

   c) to pass over.

9. "One has to be able to <u>connect</u> the past with the future." To connect means to:

   a) take apart.

   b) put together.

   c) be left alone.

1. Why were the men chopping down the dead trees?   **WHAT DO YOU THINK?**

2. Why did the men's tempers grow short?

3. Why did the men call Erik a bum?

4. Why did Erik think the men wouldn't understand?

5. Why did the adult world frighten Erik?

6. Why did his mother lie to him?

7. Why did his mother leave Denmark?

8. Why wasn't Erik accepted?

9. Why did Erik try to find himself in art?

10. Why are so many people unhappy?

1. How did men and boys wear their hair during the time of Christ?

2. What is meant by the *generation gap?*

3. What is mental health?

4. How are the mentally ill cured?

5. What does a psychiatrist do?

6. What is the subconscious?

7. Who was Sigmund Freud?

8. What is hypnotism?

9. What is shock therapy?

**WHAT IS
YOUR OPINION?**

1. What are some problems teen-agers face? Which problem do you think is the most difficult to solve?

2. Everyone wants to be liked by others. Can a person be liked by everyone? Why or why not?

JOHNNY UNITAS

The driver moved quickly.
He pressed his foot on the brake.
There was a loud screeching sound!
The big truck came to a quick stop!
Had he stopped in time? Was the boy alive?

inches from death

The people seemed frozen

"Look out!" the woman screamed. "Watch the boy's head! Stop or you'll kill him!"

People along the street stood and watched. They seemed frozen. They could do nothing. The big coal truck kept coming. It came rumbling (*RUM-bling*) down the Pittsburgh street.

The boy was gone

The driver looked for his son. He was gone! A moment ago he was sitting next to him.

The woman's words went through his mind. It hit him like a flash. It was his son the woman was screaming about! His son had fallen out of the truck.

The truck stopped

The driver moved quickly. He pressed his foot on the brake. There was a loud screeching sound. The big truck came to a quick stop.

The father ran out of his truck. He looked for his son. He saw him. His son was on the ground. The back wheel of the truck was an inch away from his head.

The boy was on the ground

The truck had stopped in time. Five year old Johnny Unitas (you-NIY-tis) was alive. One second more and he would have been killed.

One second more to live

Johnny came close to death many times. When he was seven he almost lost one leg. A bullet ripped through it. The bullet came from a shotgun. When he was older he was hurt again. It happened when he was in junior high school. He and a friend were playing with a gun. It went off. The bullet went through John's finger.

Close to death many times

Johnny felt he had a lot to be thankful for. He went to church every day. It made him feel good.

John gives thanks

Johnny's life was not easy. The Lithuanian-American had to work hard. His strong beliefs helped him. He never gave up. He fought for what he believed was right.

John grew up without a father. Mr. Unitas died when John was young. His death brought many changes. Mrs. Unitas had to be both parents. She had to care for her children. John, his older brother, and two sisters needed her.

No father in the family

Mrs. Unitas made sure of one thing. Her children would not leave school. They would not go to work without an education. She took over her husband's coal business.

Mrs. Unitas takes over

Mrs. Unitas worked hard. There was much she needed to know. She went to school. She learned bookkeeping. Her schooling helped. She could now keep the business records. In the evening, she worked as a cleaning woman. Her job helped put food on the table.

Mrs. Unitas works hard

But there was never enough money. Bills had to be paid. Food had to be bought. Clothes were needed.

Never enough money

The Unitas children learned quickly. They could not ask for money. They had to work for it.

John found a way to make money. He used his muscles. He followed coal trucks. He waited until they made their deliveries (dee-LIV-rees). Then he made his move. He grabbed his shovel. He knocked on the door. "Do you want your coal shoveled?" he would ask. "I'll do it. I'll shovel it into your cellar. I charge 75 cents a ton."

Following the coal trucks

Construction jobs   John found another way to use his muscles. He made money at the same time. He worked on construction (*kun-STRUK-shun*) jobs. His teen-age body carried heavy loads. His muscles bulged from mixing cement. His body grew stronger. It helped him when he played football.

John's dream   Football was always John's favorite sport. He had a dream. It was to someday be a football player.

It was a long, hard struggle. Being quarterback on the St. Justin's team was one thing. Being a professional player was another.

Many failures   For a time it seemed as if his dream would never come true. His tryouts ended in failure. Notre Dame and Indiana turned him down. He had a scholarship for Pittsburgh University. But he failed the entrance exam. He finally got a scholarship to Louisville College. It was a small school.

He says no   John played on the college football team. He did well. Other schools now wanted him. The big colleges asked him to transfer. He did not.

After college   After college, John tried to make a professional team. He went to many training camps. He did not make any team.

John came home. He had no money. He had to hitchhike to get back. He went back to construction work.

His wife   Many of John's friends laughed at him. But his wife did not. She stood by him. She knew football was his life.

After awhile, John began to wonder. Were his friends right? Were his football days over?

The Sunday games   Most men would have given up. John did not. He continued to play football. Each Sunday he played for a small-town team.

The telephone call   Then, one day the telephone rang. It was the Baltimore Colts. They wanted John to play for them.

The Baltimore Colts   It was a call the Colts were glad they made. Johnny Unitas became the greatest quarterback the Colts ever had.

ACTIVITIES

Johnny Unitas became a great football player because:
- **a)** his wife stood by him.
- **b)** his mother worked at night.
- **c)** he never gave up trying.
- **d)** his friends laughed at him.

DID YOU GET THE MAIN IDEA?

1. A bullet goes through John's fingers.

2. The Baltimore Colts call.

3. Indiana turns him down.

4. The truck stops inches from his head.

5. Johnny plays on St. Justin's team.

6. Johnny plays football every Sunday for a small-town team.

WHAT IS THE CORRECT ORDER?

1. John was a Lithuanian-American.

2. John's father drove a coal truck.

3. John went to Pittsburgh University.

4. John charged $1.00 a ton to shovel coal.

5. John went to church once a week.

IS IT RIGHT OR WRONG?

1. When the woman screamed, John was:
- **a)** on the ground.
- **b)** in the truck.
- **c)** on the sidewalk.

DO YOU REMEMBER?

2. The truck that came down the street was:

a) an oil truck.

b) a coal truck.

c) a milk truck.

3. When John was seven he almost lost his:

a) leg.

b) finger.

c) father.

4. John went to church:

a) everyday.

b) on Sunday.

c) once a year.

5. When Johnny was young:

a) his mother died.

b) his brother died.

c) his father died.

6. Mrs. Unitas went to school to learn:

a) English.

b) bookkeeping.

c) truck driving.

7. John made extra money by:

a) baby sitting.

b) delivering newspapers.

c) shoveling coal.

8. John's favorite sport was:

a) baseball.

b) football.

c) golf.

9. The college John went to was:
   a) Pittsburgh University.
   b) Louisville College.
   c) Notre Dame University.

10. Johnny Unitas became the quarterback for:
   a) Pittsburgh University.
   b) the Baltimore Colts.
   c) Indiana University.

1. "They seemed <u>frozen</u>." Frozen means the people:
   a) screamed.
   b) stood still.
   c) were happy.

   DO YOU KNOW THE MEANING?

2. "He pressed his foot on the <u>brake</u>." A brake makes a car:
   a) go faster.
   b) start.
   c) stop.

3. "There was a loud screeching sound." The opposite of screeching is:

   a) yelling.

   b) whispering.

   c) talking.

4. "A bullet ripped through it." To rip through means to:

   a) bounce off.

   b) miss.

   c) tear into.

5. "He waited until they made their deliveries." To deliver means to:

   a) sell.

   b) take away.

   c) bring.

6. "He grabbed his shovel." To grab means to:

   a) take.

   b) leave.

   c) look at.

7. "The big colleges asked him to transfer." To transfer means to:

   a) stay.

   b) change.

   c) return.

8. "He went to many <u>training</u> camps." When you train you:

    a) practice.

    b) teach.

    c) relax.

WHAT DO YOU THINK?

1. Why did the people in the street seem frozen?

2. Why did it make John feel good to go to church?

3. Why did Mrs. Unitas want to keep her children in school?

4. Why did John ask people if they wanted their coal shoveled?

5. Why did John need a strong body to play football?

6. Why didn't John leave the small college?

7. Why did it help John to know that his wife stood by him?

HAVE YOU EVER WONDERED?

1. How big is a football field?

2. Why is a football called a *pigskin*?

3. What are goal posts?

4. How many playing minutes are in a game of football?

5. How is coal formed?

6. What are some of the things we change coal into?

WHAT IS YOUR OPINION?

1. Have you ever worked to earn some money? What kind of work was it? Did you enjoy the work? Would you like to do that kind of work for a living?

2. Why it is important for someone in trouble to have friends or loved ones stand by him? Can you support your answer with an example from your own life?

PERMISSIONS AND PHOTO CREDITS